New Life Clarity Publishing

205 West 300 South, Brigham City, Utah 84302
Http://newlifeclarity.com/

The Right of Mercedita Noland to be identified as the Author of the work has been asserted by his/her in accordance with the Copyright Act 1988.

New Life Clarity Publishing
name has been established by NLCP.
All Rights Reserved.

No part of this publication may be reproduced, distributed, or transmitted in any form or by any means, including photocopying, recording, or other electronic or mechanical methods without the prior and express written permission of the author or publisher, except in the case of brief quotations embodied in critical reviews and certain other noncommercial uses permitted by

Printed in the United States of America

ISBN- 9781735677927
Copyright@2021 Mercedita Noland

DIAMONDS
OF WISDOM

Mercedita Noland
& Friends

ACKNOWLEDGMENTS

It is said that "a journey of a thousand miles begins with a single step". This book has been a lifelong journey for all of us who shared our "gems" of life lessons here. It certainly took great courage for me to overcome so many doubts and fears to take that single step to begin this project. My deepest gratitude to my sister-friends Annabelle Troin, Sandie Fuenty and Terri Parker for taking a tremendous leap of faith and embarking on this journey with me. Kudos and gratitude to Martina Pavlova for the exquisite and elegant cover and chapter designs without which we would have had to rely on generic templates, and that simply would not do. To Pattie Godfrey Sadler at New Life Clarity Publishing and the NLCP Editing Team who gave us the opportunity to actualize our literary vision, and for the constant encouragement each step of the way. Most of all thank you to the countless muses (spouses, mates, friends, and mentors) who have supported each of us in great and small ways. For all the mystical, magical, intangible inspirations along the way - our eternal gratitude.

Mercedita Noland

TABLE OF CONTENTS

MERCEDITA NOLAND

Chapter 1	Diamonds of Wisdom	1
Chapter 2	Conversations with Coco	7
Chapter 3	My Love Affair with Paris	15
Chapter 4	My Daily Audrey	29
Chapter 5	For the Love of Jean Luc	37
Chapter 6	Self-Confidence: Art, Manner, and Character	45
Chapter 7	The Social Mirror: A Pocket Guide to Winning Social Media Etiquette	57
Chapter 8	The VeriDiva Narrative	63
Chapter 9	My Adventure with Food	73

ANNABELLE TROIN

Chapter 10	Letter to My Younger Self	87

SANDIE FUENTY

Chapter 11	The Pink Bubble	101

TERRI PARKER

Chapter 12	The Greatest Investment	123

CHAPTER 1

DIAMONDS OF WISDOM
Sparkling Life Lessons Worth Knowing

Mercedita Noland

I have always been a dreamer, and one of my biggest dreams has been to write a book. This anthology is the fruition of that dream. Having been raised and greatly influenced by intelligent and strong-willed women has been a boon for an aspiring writer such as myself. The life lessons I learned from them were a virtual catalog of subjects that provided an infinite permutation of stories that can be shared with so many others to serve as a beacon in their life journeys.

I chose the diamond as a metaphor for the life lessons, i.e., the "gems" included in this collection, because of its many wondrous and compelling properties. The diamond is elemental, visual, visceral, spiritual, and mystical. As a near-miraculous creation of mother earth with its crystalline formation beginning as a dark solid mass of charcoal of carbon atoms, resulting from a combination of the right temperature and extreme pressure produced in the earth's lithosphere, it holds us in awe. It is as has been said in many different ways – "a diamond was a just a lump of charcoal that didn't give up under pressure". For many centuries and in many cultures including that of the Philippines, the diamond is universally acknowledged as representing light, life, purity, invincibility, fearlessness, fortitude, and perfection. It has been perpetually revered and considered as a symbol of invincible spiritual power, intellectual knowledge, treasures and riches, commitment, and faithfulness, and intuitive wisdom. Still, in many Eastern religions, diamonds are believed to have one of the **highest frequencies** that can open all chakra channels giving out healing properties – emanating from the crown or the 7th chakra believed to connect all the other chakras.

How, then, can any other symbol be more fitting?

The diamond is my birthstone. As a young girl growing up in the Philippines, it was my blessing to be part of a family tradition to receive jewelry to commemorate birthdays and other momentous occasions in one's life. I distinctly remember that for each of my birthdays, beginning at age 7, my Mother would take me to a jewelry shop named "Laperal" – a small but prestigious jewelry shop in Manila. There, we would be taken to a special presentation room by a salesperson.

The first year we went, I was to choose a necklace for my forthcoming 7th birthday. This salesperson was a formidable looking lady (who was supposedly – if rumors were to be believed - one of the twins of twin spinster sisters). She was garbed in a simple but elegant black dress, her hair tied in a chignon, black framed glasses, and no lipstick. She greeted us, her demeanor quite formal, and not a smile to indicate a warm welcome – her visage and stiff formality was a relic of Spanish and Victorian social manners. She invited us to take seats in front of a small glass table covered with black velvet, while she sat on the opposite side, and slowly proceeded to put out different pieces of diamond necklaces. She started the sales by showing us several styles of necklaces in 14 karat gold with a crucifix pendant, embellished with small diamonds - all in increasing size and with different diamond designs.

She would describe each piece with quiet technical precision and moved them around to show them to advantage. She and my mother would discuss the differences between a "diamante cut" and a "brilliant cut" and the merits and demerits of each. After several pieces, I eventually chose a gold necklace with a small crucifix encrusted with diamante cut diamonds. When I finally made my decision, the saleslady looked at me gave me an exceedingly small but authentic smile that reached her eyes! It was almost a benediction!

This was my first introduction to the joys of diamond jewelry shopping. As I got older, my fascination with diamonds continued to grow proportionately. I was forever intrigued by their origin, their mystique, their sparkling appeal and realized how life – mine in particular – is akin to this gem. I realized how so much of what truly makes us sparkle are the paths and processes that impacted us, and how we responded and conducted our lives and our relationships through these passages and how we forged a course through past trials, tribulations, heartbreaks, and victories which made us who we are – brilliant, luminescent, ineffable, and so very precious!

One of the richest lessons that I have learned has been that "no woman is an island". At the suggestion of a few good friends, I decided to invite other sister-friends to share their soul stories - the very "gems" of their own adventures (and in some cases, misadventures) to lend color, expand perspectives and bestow wisdom.

It is our earnest hope - my fellow Author friends and mine - that the stories herein serve as a glowing inspiration for you, dear readers, and may this book become one of your literary treasures!

This book is inscribed to my mother, Elizabeth Deocampo Santos. She who gave me life, who gifted me with my first diamond and who imparted to me precious life lessons that have served and still serve me well.

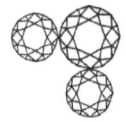

CHAPTER 2

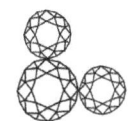

CONVERSATIONS WITH COCO

Mercedita Noland

In a beautiful and idyllic parallel universe, I would often imagine being at Angelina Paris on Rue de Rivoli. In this fantasy, I envisage that I am involved in many lively conversations with Mademoiselle Gabrielle (Coco) Chanel - over an indulgent cup of their famous hot cocoa. Everyone calls her **Mademoiselle.** Ahh…Mademoiselle - both with awe and reverence. Because she is Chanel, we are given a VIP table which is at once detached from the rest but also affords us a view of the entire floor. The patrons are elegant, the ambience opulent, the seating layout is intimate and efficient – so very French. My senses are heightened to the colors and textures of this place with its Belle Epoch and Art Deco furnishings – gilded cornices, moldings and with upholstered chairs the color of rich chocolate, that looked edible, and feels equally rich beneath my derriere.

Mademoiselle would, of course, dominate the entire

conversation in rapid French with me listening enraptured by her ideas and philosophizing - yes, in my fantasy I speak fluent French. I was actively engaged in my own fantasy where it is understood that she welcomed me as a sort of "ingénue" or "mentee", so my presence was not an intrusion of her personal time, albeit a situation she accepts perhaps with great resignation. I honestly did not care what topic she wanted to talk about on any given day – for there are many topics and issues about which Mademoiselle is extremely passionate. I was like a sponge greedy for inspiration - observing, absorbing, and in a perpetual state of osmosis.

Coco Chanel's early childhood life is shrouded in mystery because no one has ever truly discovered or at least verified the true circumstances of her childhood. There are many "myths", the most popular belief was that after her mother died, her father took her to a Catholic orphanage near Moulin's. Mademoiselle was the ultimate "queen of spin" – a smart and cunning businesswoman who carefully shaped and shared the stories that she wanted the public to know. No one asked, no one challenged it, because she is Mademoiselle! Her own version of her life story eventually became part and parcel of the Chanel ***"Mystique".***

Regardless of how this all transpired, our daily

rendezvous was filled with the most interesting and intriguing *dits*, anecdotes, chronicles of the design follies of her competitors, and even *ironic* remarks about her detractors. We, Americans would say "snide", but Mademoiselle is French, and the French are organically snide, so this is simply a matter of cultural reality. Her declaratives and gestes were all delivered emphatically and with gusto, sometimes blunt, but always with an extraordinarily strong undercurrent of a challenge. My conversations with Coco are one big caches of **challenges** – to me as a woman with great aspirations who looks up to her and to the world that still needs to evolve!

Mademoiselle on Self-esteem and Self-worth: "How many cares one loses when one decides not to be **something** but **someone**." Perhaps because of the hardships of her life and the many heartbreaks she has experienced, the softness that is wrapped very tightly in an elegant veneer of sophistication and elegance is the very essence that drove her to success. There are layers and layers of a lifetime's worth of stories in this single statement. Abandonment, loneliness, opportunities – both missed and taken, love found and lost, soul-destroying failures and triumphant successes. They all define that **someone** (**HER**)– her strength, her resilience, and that unerring belief in herself. She would sometimes sigh and have misty eyes between puffs of cigarette and a sip of cocoa (perhaps in remembrance of a particularly romantic tryst with Boy or the Duke of Westminster).

Mademoiselle on Simplicity: "Simplicity is the keynote of true elegance." Chanel's classic and timeless fashion design style is the epitome of elegance. Her indelible claim to the tenet of simplicity and elegance is absolute and indisputable. From the unconstructed (actually completely re-designed and reconstructed) "unstructured" tweed suit jacket, the repurposing of knit jersey as fashion for the aristocracy, the elevation of black and white, the camellia flower, and the simple ubiquitous **double C** logo that's ever present in every Chanel creation from pearl jewelry (always pearls), to purses, to every single gold button, and to perfume bottles that ***fashionistas*** all over the world go gaga over - the building block of her iconic brand has been simplicity. I asked her why? And she answered "Pour quoi pas?" "Why Not?"

Mademoiselle on Independence: "The most courageous act is still to think for yourself – Aloud". A volume of boldness and courage, she says this with all sass and conviction. Chanel, having attained great success and having risen phenomenally above her humble beginnings, no one questions. I believe, however, that this, the very reason she attained great success was precisely because of her boldness and innate courage. I listened and nodded and capitulated – because I agreed with her unequivocally.

Mademoiselle on Dealing with Detractors: "I don't care what you think of me, I don't think of you at all". When faced with criticism and conflict, Chanel's default attitude is to establish that who she is and her time are so valuable, and therefore, you – her detractor is not worthy of attention. I think, personally, this is the ultimate "checkmate" because you render the other party paralyzed with the very idea that she will "not engage". What a boss, huh?

Mademoiselle on Love: I had the audacity to ask her about her love life. Mademoiselle is strangely silent. This would be a conversation I think for another book. Chanel has been quoted as saying many things about men in general – one famously almost tongue-in-cheek, "If you know men are like children, you know everything". She rarely shared any details of her relationships. What we know are those told by journalists and/or reported by biographers & historians. She was infinitely famous for her well-publicized love affairs and many over-dramatized stories of her star-crossed affair with Boy Capel, or her decades-long relationship with the Duke of Winchester. Chanel was equally famous for supporting charitable causes. As she had lived her life and worked, perhaps remembering her own life journey, she gave generously, and enthusiastically, and with much ***esprit!***

My hot cocoa is finished and so is the tarte citron. Angelina is still bustling with elegant patrons. Mademoiselle finished her 3rd cigarette; she is ready to return to 31 Rue Cambon to complete what would be her last haute couture collection. This is 1971, the year she died. I imagined myself attending her funeral in my little black dress and pearls, alongside her famous contemporaries – Yves Saint Laurent, Pierre Balmain, Andre Courreges, artist Salvador Dali, and actress Jeanne Moreau, to pay our last respects.

For me – a self-declared Chanel devotee-- the conversation is far from being over.

CHAPTER 3

MY LOVE AFFAIR WITH PARIS

Mercedita Noland

My love affair with Paris began long before I went there to visit. I have read much about the City of Lights and the City of Romance.

Having read many books rhapsodizing about its allure made me dream intensely of the day when I could visit it. From these books, I remember two quotes about Paris most vividly – words that have made such an impression on me that I memorized them. I share them here because I feel that they are relevant, inspirational, and set the tone for this narrative.

The first quote is by Gertrude Stein, American novelist and playwright who said, "America is my country, but Paris is my hometown". The second quote is by George Sand – French novelist and memoirist who wrote, "I know of no other city in the world where it is more agreeable to walk along in reverie than Paris". Both women, although born nearly 70 years apart were known for their fierce independent spirits. So fierce and fearless were they that with the sheer power of their words and the way they lived their lives paved the way for many women to be elevated. They challenged the old and obsolete adages that women were weak, and therefore inferior to men. Then and now, I wholly and unequivocally support their philosophy – that women, although created differently, are equal to men.

In my lifetime, I have traveled to many countries and to many cities. I have been enthralled and wowed by many of them. Being a perpetual optimist and an inveterate romantic at heart, I always look for the beauty and charm of the place I am visiting and take pleasure from each place's individual charms and enjoy them to the hilt. No other city, however, has captured my imagination, nor can compare to the nearly indescribable bliss I experience whenever I am in the "City of Lights". Paris appeals to and resonates with me on so many levels. This resonance is at once sensual and intellectual, buoyant, and melancholic, flamboyant, and cerebral and always, always provocative, and profound!

Fall 1989 was my first visit – when I first "showed up" in Paris. It was love at first sight! I was invited as part of an incentive trip for travel coordinators (one of my main responsibilities working for a multi-national company) -- to see and to experience the city. The trip was sponsored by Air France and its related hotel properties. The invitation was for a 6-day all expenses paid trip that included business-class and first-class round-trip air fare, luxury hotel accommodations at Le Meridien Montparnasse and Le Meridien Étoile, tours and meals! The invitation came at a time when I was financially broke and emotionally broken.

Having been recently divorced, uprooted from my beautiful home, and forced to move to a different city with my three-year-old son, I was a woman in deep survival mode. And despite my "default" attitude to look brave and bright, I was crying inside. This was one of the reasons I demurred from accepting the first time I was invited. I had no spare funds for a trip anywhere, least of all for a trip to Paris! In the end, gracious pressure was exerted for me to decide because timely arrangements had to be made with both Air France and Le Meridien hotels. After much painful deliberation and successfully arranging for my son to be watched by my Great Aunt Flor (who encouraged me to go), I finally said Yes!

That year, the Eiffel Tower was celebrating its centennial year. She was 100 years old. Every night that I was there, it was lit up in all its glory, so beautiful and so scintillating. In the quiet hours of the night, when my life's challenges fully hit me, the Eiffel Tower became for me a beacon of hope – quite literally and metaphorically. She has endured and so shall I.

During the "free days" when we were not required to travel as a group, I walked all over the city, traversed the streets of the Left Bank or "La Rive Gauche" and the Right Bank or "La Rive Droite" of the Seine – the river that divides Paris. During these walks and, as George Sand had written, I was utterly lost in reverie! I went both in the daytime and nighttime. Sometimes alone, and sometimes with 2 of the guys who were in my tour group – John and Paolo. At one of our solo jaunts, John and Paolo "confessed" to me that they were gay. When I simply raised an eyebrow and unshockingly and unperturbedly asked them, "And your point is?" They immediately granted me their friendship and loyalty and adopted me as a surrogate sister of sorts.

We walked and found adventure everywhere! The Right Bank or "La Rive Droite" is also known "posh Paris" – fashionable, attractive and with the famous Avenue des Champs Elysees, Avenue Montaigne and the Place Vendome, represented all the "joie de vive" that France is known for. This is where all the haute couture and globally iconic design houses such as Chanel, Dior, Louis Vuitton, and Hermes – brands that are synonymous to French elegance - are located. Many of the ladies in the group shopped at these designer boutiques, where I would not even dare go inside because I knew I would not be able to afford anything! I distinctly remember our beautiful host, Isabel, purchased a gorgeous crystal vase from the House of Baccarat. She hand-carried this treasure on the plane with her all the way home. It was a singularly stunning work of art that represented to me something to aspire to. I promised myself that the next time I visit Paris, I will be able to afford and purchase a piece of Baccarat crystal.

Here at Rive Droite also are the Louvre Museum where 3 days is not enough to soak up the entirety of the story of the world's civilization, the Pantheon – the penultimate monument to the French nation's democracy that loudly proclaims "Liberty, Equality and Brotherhood" on its front facade and, of course, the Palais Garnier and the Bastille Opera – the 2 most prestigious theaters in the world.

The Left Bank is what I call the "Artsy, Intellectual Paris". Historically known for nurturing the creative (and often tortured) souls of literary legends such as Ernest Hemmingway, Henry Miller, Anais Nin, and Gertrude Stein, to name a few. It is where, for decades, street artists performed on the streets for tokens practically every day of the week.

The Right Bank and the Left Bank are the geographical representations of the cultural paradox that is Paris! Along its boulevards and cafes are an untold number of soul-stirring stories – lived and created by its inhabitants and the expatriates who are drawn there like bees to honey.

As earlier mentioned, at the time of my first Paris trip, I was a newly divorced, broke, emotionally unravelling and a struggling single mother of a three-year-old son. I accepted a position with a fair-sized company as an administrative assistant. One of my main tasks was as travel coordinator – a position far below my skill set and educational attainment – where one of my daily responsibilities was to arrange and coordinate all the travel requirements for the company's top and mid-level executives. I was in deep survival mode reeling from a violent breakup of a marriage that I thought would last forever and struggling emotionally and financially.

My job provided me with enough money to pay for my cost of living while raising a child, but by no means did I have any extra for any kind of luxury. When the Paris trip offer was made, I eventually accepted realizing that it was an opportunity I might never have again. It was one of the best decisions of my life because I finally met a city that embraced me in all my brokenness, all my yet unfulfilled dreams, all my promise, and all my potential for greatness!

Fast Forward to the Spring 2009, exactly 20 years

later, a million other stories of struggles and triumphs in between, I have attained a moderate amount of success as a financial advisor. I got engaged to Rod - a lovely man who has been my best friend for 7 years before we became romantically involved. After living together for 5 years, he presented me with a beautiful diamond ring and he and I agreed to exchange vows in Paris! We booked our plane, paid for our hotel in advance, and through a dear friend of mine, Sister Nenita Patena – arranged for a wonderful Catholic Priest, Father Marcelo Manimtim - to bless our vows!

After all these arrangements, we belatedly found out that couples are required to live in France for at least 60 days to be granted a marriage license! My fiancé and I looked at each other, said "bleep" the license, we are going ahead with our plans without an official marriage license! We exchanged vows on a beautiful spring day at the Luxembourg Gardens, surrounded by centuries-old sculptures and monuments to saints and the countless botanical marvels the gardens are known for. Our intimate ceremony was witnessed by our two gay friends – Roger and Edwin - my very own "Gays of Honor". Afterwards, we went for a delicious lunch and champagne and in the evening celebrated at the George V, Four Seasons Paris.

We spent 10 glorious days in Paris, mostly reprising

the things I did when I visited in 1989, as well as visiting the places I did not get to see. We made special memories just for our post-vows-exchange! We walked around the Trocadero, visited the Eiffel Tower, spent an afternoon there where we met a nice old lady named Jeannette at a café kiosk at the park. I gave Jeannette a bar of Nestle chocolate crunch which she opened slowly and with such elan, savored with such gusto with her cup of coffee. She told us she is a grandmother of 4 and lives not a mile from the park.

Every morning, my Sweetheart would get up and go to the nearby café, picked up café au lait and croissants and bring them back to our room. After about a week of that, he made friends with the café owner – Pierre, who told him where the best local places to eat were. We followed each of his recommendations and it was well worth the adventure. We attended a Sunday solemn high mass at the Notre Dame Cathedral, a service conducted in 3 languages – French, English, and Latin! Afterwards, we had lunch at Ile Saint Louis followed by standing in a long line to Bartholomew's for a taste of the world's most famous ice cream.

We bought a day-pass to the Louvre, where I met an 8-year-old boy who was on a field trip with his class. We were both checking out the "fountain of Medusa", an enormous red granite fountain dating over 500 years with a fearsome bronze sculpture of Medusa at the center. In my rudimentary French, I explained to him that Medusa was a mythical figure whose eyes turned you into stone. The little wretch looked at me with all the arrogance of a prince and told me in perfect English, "I know, Madame – I am French." I was so flabbergasted by the response – I think I was simultaneously impressed as well as shocked by his attitude, so I simply raised my right eyebrow and dryly said, "Good for you." Afterwards, I recounted this to anyone who would listen and had a great laugh! Father Marcelo said that the "French do take great pride in their children's education". So, really Kudos to them!

Rod and I went on our own for a day trip to Versailles (his first and my second visit). This time, I served as Rod's tour guide and explained things to him while we walked through the Palace of Versailles Senate Room, the Queen's chamber, and the Hall of Mirrors which provided a remarkable view of the gardens outside.

We walked in great wonder and admiration around this beautiful garden with its parterres, trees, orangery, groves, and priceless sculptures. I, of course took lots and lots of photographs for posterity. The spectacular garden whose design and renovation were entrusted by Louis XIV to the famous architect, Andre Le Notre is a living legacy of France's glorious (and violent) history.

We walked, browsed, ate and of course, shopped. We shopped everywhere – at the "festival des arts creatifs" where many artists and artisans proudly sell their wares and attended by many American store buyers who were on the hunt for fresh designs and fresh talents. This is where I met a lovely artist named Chloe who designed gorgeous hats and fascinators. I did not want a hat, but I fell in love with a large hand-made silk flower in fuchsia! I asked her if I could just purchase the flower because I needed to wear one in my hair. She agreed, she took it out of the hat and created a beautiful hair piece right before my eyes. In her own words, "it has to be perfect"! I still have that silk flower and have worn it on my hair and as a brooch on many special occasions! It still looks as fresh and beautiful as the day I purchased it!

It is important to note that by this time, I can afford pretty much anything, and so at one of our shopping expeditions, we went to the Baccarat boutique at Les Printemps where I purchased a Baccarat crystal wine carafe – a promise made to myself in 1989, now kept. I also indulged in Mariage Freres teas, purchased a dozen glossy tins to give to tea-loving friends in the States, as well as bags and bags of luxurious and heavenly smelling "Orchidee de Minuit" (Midnight Orchid) bath salts wrapped in elegant silver-grey bags with silver ribbons and silver Eiffel Towers Charms, for special girlfriends. These bath salts were made from pure midnight orchid essential oil such that the luggage I brought them in smelt of the fragrance for months!

Since that time, I have been to Paris 2 more times – in 2015 with my friend, Annabelle, to celebrate our milestone birthdays (with a 5-day London trip prior), and in 2016, for a combined vacation and wedding celebration of my one and only son to my precious daughter-in-law!

The year 2015 represented to me what I dub as **my year of becoming**! Having achieved success in my profession as a financial advisor and having successfully raised a wholesome, healthy, and wonderful son, this year marked for me the beginning of the next chapter of my life. When I was no longer responsible (at least financially) for my child as he has completed his college education and is professionally situated, I decided that now, I will focus on every dream, every goal I had long ago set for myself and put aside during my years of living in "survival mode". I am now in "success mode".

During this trip, we stayed at one of the most iconic 5-star hotels in Paris - Le Royal Monceau Paris. We were accommodated in a special suite with a "salle de bain avec miroirs sans ombres" or a suite with a "bathroom with mirrors that have no shadows". This was designed by French architect Philippe Starck – who is famous for his elegant and utopian ideal of creating and designing interiors and various useful everyday items not just for the upper-crust, but for everyone. This suite, in and of itself, was an architectural and technological wonder. Somehow, the room temperature and the lighting were always perfect, regardless of the weather outside, or the time of day. Our suite overlooked a compact but elegant patio adjacent to the Michelin starred restaurant, Il Carpaccio, where we had our dinner the first night we arrived. It was framed by boxes of colorful flowers. The suite was a perfect marriage of utility and luxury, and the perfect place to inhabit after full days of shopping, dining, and sightseeing.

We made friends with the Lady Concierge, Margaux, who was literally our personal go-to lady during our stay there. Margaux was the quintessential French woman – she was slim, elegant, and was very gracious to us.

I fulfilled another promise to myself – I purchased expensive luxuries such as my first Chanel necklace and first Fendi purse at the boutiques in Avenue Montaigne and a one-of-a-kind Italian silk scarf with 3 kinds of fur on the collar from Leclaireur. As of this writing, I celebrated yet another milestone birthday, but no matter where I am in life, Paris will always represent the fulfillment of promises I made to myself – the most important promises to keep.

CHAPTER 4

MY DAILY AUDREY

Mercedita Noland

Every young girl is a dreamer, whether she was raised on a farm or a dyed-in-the-blue city girl like me. Every dreamer has a constant muse. I am the quintessential dreamer, and my constant Muse is Audrey Hepburn. Audrey represented to me all that was beautiful, elegant, chic, fashionable, feminine, and gracious. As a young woman and through adulthood, I watched her movies – "Roman Holiday", "Breakfast at Tiffany's", "Sabrina", "How to Steal a Million", "Charades" and even the thriller "Wait Until Dark" dozens of times and never tired of them. Something about Audrey's aura attracts and compels us to watch, observe and emulate. She has an undefinable quality that is both visually alluring and at the same time mystifyingly real.

Growing up in a cosmopolitan city like Manila and with a family who loved theater and the arts, going to the movies was one fun activity that was always available and permitted among my siblings and me. Weekends and school holidays, I would go to the movie theater with girlfriends and for about an hour or two, we would be swept up in the story and the drama that unfolds on the big screen! My friends and I would allocate a portion of our "milk money" to watch Audrey Hepburn movies. After each movie, we would discuss passionately - with a fervor that young females are capable of - and endlessly, how we would transform our wardrobes to be as chic and as trendy as Holly Golightly's or Sabrina's!

I remember watching "Breakfast at Tiffany's" for the first time on the big screen. I could never forget the opening scene with Audrey alighting from an iconic yellow New York taxi, wearing a long black gown, up-do, statement pearl necklace and a tiara! Even now, as I imagine it, I can remember that thrill and excitement growing while watching as the camera pans over the fashionable street and follows her elegant back to stop in front of Tiffany's with a white paper bag and coffee. Henry Mancini's "Moon River" sans the lyrics rendered in violins! It is an image too special not to loop in one's head!

I was too young, innocent, and too naïve to recognize the subtext of the story, yet I was drawn to the personal traits of the main protagonist played by Audrey. I only ever saw it as a romantic story and my consciousness was only ever focused on the idea and the ideal of having that kind of feminine freedom; that "Nothing bad can ever happen to you at Tiffany's"; and fully, unquestionably believing that going there was the best panacea for getting a grip when you get the "Mean Reds" because "There will be days when you will be angry or afraid and you won't be able to pin down exactly what's bothering you". That having an animal in your life, regardless of your bank account, means "pure love". Perhaps, the story's best lesson of all is that finding someone who knows you and loves you with all your flaws is equivalent to finding true happiness.

"Sabrina" of course forever and indelibly told me that "Paris is always a good idea". Once again, the plot was a bit too mature for me when I first saw the movie, but once again, I only felt the romanticism of it and ultimately the elegance of her transformation from a chauffer's daughter to a fashionable young lady with marketable skills and now fully endowed with all the glamor and panache she learned as an intern at Vogue Paris! Sigh!

Many decades and over a dozen Audrey movies watched over a thousand times later, I find myself a mature woman with a successful career and a thriving, elite women's business networking group. Established based on the principle of transformational relationship networking, one of our main precepts is the principle of giving back. And once more, my Muse found me, or perhaps more accurately, I re-discovered my Muse, Audrey. Beyond the glamorous Hollywood icon and the ultra-chic Givenchy gowns – there was Audrey the humanitarian. Her work as Ambassador of the United Nations International Children's Fund (UNICEF) deeply inspired me to find a cause that would uplift the plight of children.

The million-dollar questions were: Which children's charity and in which country? Having learned from many articles, that many children in developing countries were living below the poverty level, dying of starvation and malnutrition, dying from famine and drought, dying because they are not getting proper medical attention, or getting killed in acts of insidious terrorism. Thus, my search began. In 2009, the inspiration presented itself when I watched the Oscars and Megan Mylan won the Oscar for "Best Documentary Short" for her 39-minute documentary film entitled, "Smile Pinki".

The film was about the plight of a poor girl (Pinki) born with cleft lip, who lived in rural India and how her life was transformed when she received free cleft repair surgery. I watched the movie and my heart cried for this little girl and learning that there were millions more children born with cleft, my heart broke some more, and I cried and cried some more.

Time to act.

Audrey's humanitarian work was her most profound legacy. In a tribute letter written by Robert Wolders, her long-time companion, he said that Audrey believed that every child is a "universe of potential, with the inherent right to live in a world that protects and nurtures that potential". I wholeheartedly agree!

Audrey has become our very own "mascot" for supporting Smile Train – a children's charity that provides free cleft lip and cleft palate repair surgeries to underserved children in more than 88 of the world's developing countries. Since 2009, I have become a staunch supporter of this worthy charity. I strongly believe in its core value that a cleft repair surgery's impact is "immediate" and "permanent". They train local doctors on how to operate on the children and these doctors often donate their time and skills, hence a large portion of the funds pay for travel, hospital stay and necessary medicines.

The fact that more than 85% of donated funds directly benefit the child being sponsored rather than being spent on research and administrative costs, also appeals to me as a financial professional – yes, I liked their numbers and I love the idea of giving these children a second chance at life!

I have always said that we never know which of these children would be the next Albert Einstein or the next Gandhi! Children with cleft have innate intelligence, but their opportunities to learn and develop are severely handicapped by this condition.

In many countries, a mother can have a first child born with cleft and succeeding children without a cleft and vice versa. In many countries both the mother and child are ostracized because of the child's deformities. Beyond the mother's inability to feed her baby is the inherent hopelessness of growing with this curable condition. This fact alone solidified my decision to support Smile Train.

Every year, for the past 10 years, since I founded our organization, we have hosted various fundraisers, to raise funds and awareness to benefit Smile Train. It is one activity that utterly lifts our souls and elevates our spirits! Indeed, we believe that each child we sponsor is a "Smile Earned in heavenly indulgences"! Our efforts have become even more intensely needed during the Covid-19 pandemic.

Over the years, we have adopted Audrey's "I Believe in Pink" motto as our "theme and inspirational manifesto" for creating fun, classy and memorable fundraising events! Audrey's eternal and enduring class, style and elegance never fail to effortlessly attract others to join and support our fundraising efforts. We have anchored our charitable goals to Audrey's universal and emblematic appeal for compassion and kindness and it has served us well.

For the non-believers, we share with you Audrey's Manifesto.
We believe it will inspire you, too:

I believe in Pink.
I believe that laughing is the best calorie burner.
I believe in kissing. Kissing a lot.
I believe in being strong when
everything seems to be going wrong.
I believe that Happy Girls are the Prettiest Girls.
I believe that Tomorrow is another day and
I believe in Miracles.

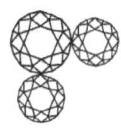
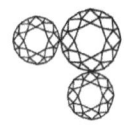

CHAPTER 5

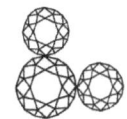

FOR THE LOVE OF JEAN LUC

Mercedita Noland

"*When I grow up, I'd like to be the kind of person my dog thinks I am.*" This was the plaque prominently hung in the first vet's office where I took Jean Luc. The plaque was right next to a floor-to-ceiling *Gratitude Wall* where photos of all sizes and breeds of canines and felines and notes from their grateful owners were proudly posted. I took that message from the plaque to heart and have been working to be "that kind of person".

Jean Luc, who is my precious **Malte-Pek** is a love-gift from my fiancé, Rod. His sire was a pure-bred Pekingese, and his mother was a pure-bred Maltese. We acquired him in 2011 – a decision made after 12 years of lively discussions on the pros and cons of adding a canine to our family. There were many "cons" as we are both wanderlusts and loved to getaway as often as possible. In the end the "pros" won. He was the runt of the second litter, was 4 weeks old and two and half lbs. He had soft white hair all over, with a strip of fawn beige color running from his crown to his shoulder. He had mostly Maltese features, but with a slight under-bite from the Pekingese side. He fitted in the palm of my hand - puny but he already exhibited a huge personality. As soon as we took him home, I prepared a small basket lined with the finest, softest Egyptian cotton towel for him to sleep in and he promptly got out and slept next to us in our bed. He has been sleeping in our bed ever since.

For all intents and purposes, Jean Luc is our canine-child – with all the responsibilities that having a child entail. Having each raised a child, we were literally empty nesters who thoroughly loved the freedom. Acquiring him meant adjusting our lifestyle to an exponential degree. Pre-Jean Luc, we traveled at the drop of a hat, to whatever destination we wanted to go. For as long as my professional commitments were "covered" and did not have any face-to-face client meetings, we took off – for a week, 2 weeks, or longer. We did not have to check if the hotel and the surrounding restaurants were dog-friendly, nor did we have to search for trustworthy puppy-sitters/house-sitters to stay with him if we had out-of-town family commitments that cannot accommodate having him with us. Jean Luc has never stayed in a kennel – because neither Rod nor I can handle that.

Both of Jean Luc's parents were owned by our neighbors who lived right next door, and when I used to take him to our backyard to do his rituals, he would often afterwards just sit in front of the fence staring and I know he knew his parents were just on the other side of the fence. This went on for months and each time, my heart went out to him. A month into our owning him, he got sick with Parvo-like symptoms – high fever, lack of appetite, lack of energy, and teary eyed. There was a huge outbreak of the Parvo virus that killed hundreds of dogs during this time. We took him to the vet, who gave him a number of prescriptions. I prayed so hard for him to be spared. He was.

For the past nine years that we have nurtured and cared for Jean Luc, we have been "Puppy Mommy" and Puppy Daddy". In return, he taught us the ideals of unconditional love and devotion. He is fiercely protective and devoted to both of us, albeit shows his affection to each of us in two very distinct ways. Whenever I come home – whether it was after 3 hours or 3 days, he would let me pick him up and **howl** like he was literally dying – this to express that he missed me and that I should not have left for so long. For to him, my absence was absolute, and the length of time was irrelevant – I was missed. Full Stop. Period. I would then assure him that I am back and will be home for the duration of the day. When Puppy Daddy comes home – he jumps up at him and gives his face and hands "kiss-licks" to let him know he has been missed!

Jean Luc relates to us highly intuitively. Once, I learned that a very dear friend died, and I started crying quietly in my office. He came, stood on his hind legs, and asked me to pick him up. He promptly put his front paws on my shoulders and kissed my face as if to say, "Don't cry Puppy Mommy". I, of course, cried even more – touched that this little creature somehow understood my grief. There have also been many times when I have been sick, he would just lay by my feet or on the floor by the couch in "sympathy".

They say that "play is good for the soul". If that is the case, then every day, our souls are happily nourished because Jean Luc wakes us up. He just sits right next to either one of us and stares until we are conscious enough to feel and acknowledge that he is right there, or if we are especially in deep sleep, he would gently tap his paws to our cheeks until we wake up. He would then start licking our hands and faces. When we tell him it is time to get up, he will typically engage us in a bout of wrestling and *catch-catch me if you can* for several minutes until he is ready to be picked up. We have learned to make time for play – to surrender to the pure innocence and unadulterated joy of just being and doing nothing especially productive – or but perhaps it is.

Because canines evolved from wolves, Jean Luc considers every human who comes into his life on a more-or-less regular basis to be part of his *pack*. He acknowledges each one with unreserved joy and lets them know they matter to him. He guards his menagerie of stuffed animals as if they were his own pups. When he is given a treat that he does not eat, he puts them in "secret places" among his menagerie. He loves pretty women and every single lady who visits is subjected to the patented Jean Luc charm. He kisses them, sits with them, and engages with them. He would often turn back to look at me and I would assure him that "I'm not jealous" and he would continue charming them.

Last year, our neighbor's 120 lb. English Mastiff – Taffy - got out from their house and bounded up to Jean Luc and me while we were in the front yard. I have no way of ever knowing if she was just eager to play because she started mauling Jean Luc and Jean Luc being the protector that he is started to counter-attack. I tried to carry him, but he was so strong his harness got unlatched and he ran to our front door. I cried for help, but there was no one. I fell hard on my knees trying to shoo away the other dog, but to no avail. In the back of my mind, I was also afraid that she might turn on me. I followed them to the front door, all the while shooing her away from Jean Luc. When I reached them, she was on top of Jean Luc who is all of 17 lbs. I saw blood on Jean Luc's face and the look in his eyes that said, "**Puppy Mommy, please help me**!" As strong a woman as I thought I was, I have never ever felt so helpless and so desperately futile than at that moment.

In the end, and perhaps simply **by Divine Grace**, Taffy got off Jean Luc and left. We promptly took him to the Emergency Pet Hospital. They took tests and saw several deep abrasions and dark heavy bruising, but miraculously the blood on his face was not his, and he had no facial or head wounds. The Vet concluded that the blood belonged to the other dog – which meant Jean Luc had hurt her enough for her to change her mind and leave. I was deeply traumatized by this incident and profoundly grateful that he survived. Another experience that taught me how precious life is and how precious Jean Luc has become to us.

Jean Luc's Puppy Daddy has a group of retirees who meet for coffee every morning at the local Starbucks. Over the years, Jean Luc has become their unofficial mascot - definitely *one of the boys*! He continues to be a large and loving aspect of our family dynamics, and we both believe that Jean Luc has helped to make us better people and better mates.

This past May, Jean Luc turned 9 years old. Thousands of "family pictures", trips to the vets and groomers, family dramas, many happy occasions, and his very own Pinterest Page later, we continue to love and be loved. As a family, we have visited many, many places and patronized numerous businesses that are dog friendly. We have also made deep and lasting connections with other Puppy Parents who are as devoted to their canine children as we are. It is an incredibly special club – this parenthood of canines-humans-parents, and the only main requirements are love and devotion.

I have always had an affinity with canines, having had dogs in my family even as a child, but I never related to any single one as I have related to Jean Luc. They were "family animals" – fed and cared for, but I never knew them on a one-on-one basis the way I learned to relate with and care for Jean Luc and to have a deeper understanding of life. I believe I am a more compassionate human being because of this. I am still growing and still evolving into the "kind of person my dog thinks I am" – the edict is still up, and only time will tell. For now, there is only love.

CHAPTER 6

SELF-CONFIDENCE: ART, MANNER, AND CHARACTER

Mercedita Noland

What exactly is *Self-Confidence*? I turned to Webster Thesaurus and looked it up. There are so many synonyms for Confidence – *self-assurance, poise, self-possessed, classy, elegant, upbeat, serene, unshaken, tranquil, rosy, and sanguine*! Wow! I think that Confidence is all this and more. One of the basic tenets of confidence is *subtlety* – in poise and manner and behavior without excessive expression. Otherwise, confidence, which is universally perceived as a positive and appealing trait simply becomes deemed as arrogance.

I begin with the premise that Self-Confidence is something that is cultivable. It is one of those game-changing habits that I believe is a pre-requisite to real success - authentic, organic, and ultimately wholly gratifying.

Having experienced alienation and bullying in my early childhood and adolescence and having my sense of self-worth seemingly irreparably damaged, regaining self-confidence was a hard-won behavior dynamic for me. As a child, I excelled academically, and I know without any false modesty or conceit that I am intellectually gifted. I was also equally outgoing and always ready to help a classmate having difficulty with their studies. And yet despite this – or in retrospect perhaps because of this – some of my classmates were quite mean and cruel. There were also family members who made certain remarks that were quite damaging such as "you're not as fair or as pretty as your cousins," or "it's a good thing you're smart". The implication of not being enough unless one is "pretty" was always ever hanging overtly. You might say I had a double-whammy of negative reinforcements that made me feel inadequate – facts that unerringly challenged my self-confidence and self-worth. The scars were deep.

Fortunately, I have strong women who were great role models and who balanced these negative onslaughts to my emotional and psychological development. I also possessed the IQ to question and rebel at how awful these experiences and how mean and cruel these people were to me. And rebel I did! I rebelled by relentlessly studying and observing what makes a person, especially a woman Confident? What made her look elegant? I asked my elders, teachers, and anyone else who cared to pay attention, why certain people have so much poise. More importantly, **how did they attain that wondrous state of being?** So I began to observe the women in my family, family friends who visited, teachers and women in history, film, and art. I had a treasure trove of role models upon which to build.

The evolution of this undertaking is quite interesting . It is also funny in many instances and proved quite fulfilling as I matured. I tackle this often-elusive characteristic and behavior dynamic with a pragmatic attitude. I aim to hopefully deconstruct it in such a way that the end result is beyond the "fake it 'til you make it" mentality and enable others to develop and grow into Self-Confidence organically and authentically, to behave with ease, being comfortable in her own skin, to radiate from within and resonate outwardly. To be "ALL THAT" without the requisite artifice and often obvious and cringe-worthy ways people attempt to compensate for its lack.

The Art of Confidence:

Firstly, I consider the concept of Self-Confidence as *Art* because it is, I believe, the simplest and easiest perspective. The dictionary defines Art as the expression or application of human creative skill and imagination… *typically in visual form.* Art is likewise considered as a vehicle for the *expression* or communication of *emotions* and ideas. We see the way supremely confident people walk, talk, and most importantly how thy communicate and relate with others. We simply see and perceive their confidence, poise, and elan.

But Hold It! Is it really that simple? The answer is a resounding No!

As a woman growing up in the 60's and the 70's, there was a minefield of confusing visual aesthetics, sub-cultures, and political trends that one had to navigate and to hopefully transcend unscathed. The prevailing fashion in clothes, the explosion of the "Love Generation" and hippie movement and the resurgence of the Equal Rights Amendment were all powerful influences on one's self-confidence. They were all equally empowering and polarizing!

Where did I land? In college, the inner struggle continued, but I consciously suppressed it by focusing on getting educated and starting a career – all I wanted was to be independent! I read books that increasingly fed my desire to see the world while having independent means of doing so. I became intimate with Karl Jung, Sigmund Freud, Ayn Rand and even Jacquelin Susann and Harrold Robbins. My sense of fashion also changed as I became more conscious of what my peers were wearing – miniskirts, bell bottoms, shiny patent boots and apple-cut hair dos. In between semesters, I got summer sales jobs that I genuinely enjoyed! I was 18 when I got my first summer job, but I lied to my employers and told them I was 21. I earned money way more than my school allowance and experienced the joy of having and spending my own money and the ability to purchase what I wanted without asking for my parents' permission. Here was my earliest experience of *financial ability as a building block of self-confidence.*

Fast forward to the late 70's and early 80's. Over a period of 9 years, I got hired by 3 great companies in succession! And in each succession, as my earning capability rose, my self-confidence increased proportionately. The observation and due diligence to develop self-confidence continued, however, with a seriously significant layer of **_Independence_**! Yes, bolded, italicized and underscored!

I thoroughly enjoyed the social scene - hanging out, dinner parties with my fellow workmates and dated – socially (read as no romantic sub-text). I was mainly focused on building my career, travelling, and going abroad. I had absolutely no intention of getting married! As my earning capability grew, I also felt more confident. I followed the latest trends in fashion, indulged in designer clothing and accessories, and circulated in the best circles. *The Art perfected!*

The Manners: A way in which a thing is done or happens. A person's outward bearing or way of behaving toward others.

I remember that from elementary school through college, we had required subjects such as "Etiquette" and "GMRC" or Good Manners and Right Conduct. These courses were supposed to serve as a "finishing courses" to polish us for when we were ready to go to the outside world and prepare to tackle a career. We were taught how to walk properly, how to make proper social introductions, how to answer a phone call in a professional environment, how to walk straight, how to set and eat at a formal table and how to dress for specific occasions – pointed high heels and nylon stockings were very much involved. To be perfectly honest, I can remember all of these with much fondness because my classmates and I giggled endlessly during these classes – much to the chagrin of our instructors. I remember all the social niceties, but I cannot recall the "Right Conduct" part. It almost felt like the entire course was dedicated to the outward trappings but did not ever address (or even pretend to) the meanness of character (or correcting it) that was just under the surface for certain people.

As I became more successful career-wise, more socially adept, and as my financial blunt grew, I became more self-confident. Having beautiful and successful friends enhanced my sense of social acceptance. Ironically, because I was not interested in getting hitched, I ended up dating extraordinarily successful men who were somehow attracted to me. Sub-consciously, I asked myself why? But did not genuinely care about the answer because I was not interested in any of them romantically. I understood from a purely objective frame of reference that I had to be outwardly appealing and socially acceptable, therefore dressing well was a necessity. It was simply that – a means to an end. I made especially important social and professional connections that subsequently enhanced my awareness of the importance of self-confidence.

During this time, and with my parents being blissfully unaware, I also aligned myself with the concept of sexual equality that women may do as they please with whom they pleased without the benefit of marriage. I was "liberated" but not promiscuous. For a Catholic-bred young woman, this is a major rebellion with serious psychological challenges, and I would most emphatically offer a serious *caveat* to any young woman.

Something is missing! I continued to read and searched for spiritual answers and fed my curiosity on the path to enlightenment. I read Og Mandino, Lao Tsu, Frederick Nietzsche (who by the way was given an awfully bad rep by our Theology professors), Ralph Waldo Emerson, the transcendental movement and David Hume. I fed my intellect and it, in turn, fed me. My conversations were always a little bit esoteric for many of my friends, but as a result, I also made deep and lasting friendships with people who "got me". One of my longest-standing friendships is with Sister Nenita Patena, who blessedly unconditionally loves me and accepts me for who and what I am. Because of this friendship, I began to accept me for who I am – quirky, intelligent, and unique. I behaved less brashly perhaps, I developed a more open attitude, allowed myself to trust more and accepted that there will be people who likes me for who I am and that there will be people who will not.

Manners perfected? Not Quite!

Character Development and Self-Confidence: Character is defined as the mental and moral qualities distinctive to an individual.

I take great literary license on the title of this topic because character includes self-confidence. To round up a total person's being is to include both her personality traits and her character. It is interesting to note that the definition of the word "character" is always attached to the word "moral" and vice versa. Thus, if we were to address a person's standards of behavior concerning her belief of what is right and prudent, we would essentially call it a person's moral character. This, to me is the most challenging aspect in the development of one's Self-Confidence. Does having good moral character equal Self-Confidence? Conversely, does Self-Confidence enhance one's moral character?

The eternal questions of what is [doing] what is morally right (*proper*) vs. morally wrong (*improper*) continues to plague our society. It continues to be in the forefront of my consciousness. As I developed the more apparent aspects of my self-confidence – refinement of social behavior, attaining self-sufficiency and financial independence, I also felt the challenge to prove my mettle as a Leader – both in my personal relationships as well as in my professional relationships.

In late 2019, a revered Professional Power Coach once asked me on a scale of 1 to 10, how I would rate myself as a Leader and where would I like to be. I answered boldly and without hesitation that I considered myself a "9" and I would like to be a "10"; I also told him that I fully realized that reaching that would take an epic "quantum leap" on my part – because I am my biggest work-in-progress project!

As a long-term Financial Advisor, I have had to master

the art of communication, of selling intangibles – the idea of attaining financial security, peace of mind and dignity in old age – all part and parcel of my career development. The biggest challenge is developing patience. I am confident in my abilities and in my recommendations, but I must constantly and consistently transcend my clients' fears of loss and overcoming their aversion to taking risks.

As Founder and C.E.O. of an elite women's business networking group, I have had to develop the kind of Self-Confidence required to stir and navigate a difficult business dealing in "transformational relationships". I have had to make and continue to make exceedingly difficult decisions to propel my organization onwards to serve its goal to encourage, educate and empower other women. Over the past 10 years, I have had to take several steps back to see where things could be significantly improved. There have been countless instances when my Self-Confidence (along with my integrity) was severely challenged and when I have had to revert to the "Manners" part of this Self-Confidence evolution and behave with strength, fairness, and gravitas.

A few years ago, my son posted a short Instagram Mother's Day tribute to me – he said, "Happy Mother's Day to the woman who taught me about vision, hustle and keeping it classy." I will take it because I consider this is one of my life's most precious and priceless tributes – it underscores how far my Self-Confidence has evolved! To have been a mother and to have raised a healthy, wholesome human being is the ultimate validation.

I would like to conclude by saying that dipping my ink and toes in the complex issues of self-confidence has been a tremendous work. I want to say that I hope we all learn to understand and realize that Self-Confidence is part of our DNA. It is an innate gift that we oftentimes "lose" along the way. Be not discouraged dear friends, because that feeling of "losing self-confidence" is just an *illusion*; because one cannot really lose what is innate, and because we only need to look inwards to find it waiting for us to re-discover. Oftentimes – as in my own life - we must look a little deeper.

But we must be committed to do the work - to improve our minds, bodies, and spirits. To have the courage to let go and decide who is worth keeping relationships with, to pursue that which makes us happy, to contribute in any small way to the betterment of our community and per chance to leave a worthy legacy. I confidently declare that we all have the ability to develop and manifest effervescent and radiant Self-Confidence!

CHAPTER 7

THE SOCIAL MIRROR: A POCKET GUIDE TO WINNING SOCIAL MEDIA ETIQUETTE

Mercedita Noland

According to Stephen Covey, author of *"The 7 Habits of Highly Effective People",* the social mirror is a metaphor for the way we see ourselves because others reflect their perceptions, opinions and paradigms about us through their words and behaviors." From this social mirror, we form images and judgments of ourselves (e.g. "I'm not a creative person" or "I'm good with numbers").

GOOD Social Media Etiquette is perceived as a positive and constructive social mirror. I learn as I do and this is intended mostly to serve as a "guideline" particularly for many of us, professional women, who share both our personal and business lives on social media.

BRANDING ON 5G – OMG!

Remember that Social Media is a Significant and Important Form of Communication. What you share, express, post, like, love, care, and who you follow and engage with, is a direct reflection of your own emotional, intellectual, and psychological makeup. It shows to others your interests, your passion, your goals and even your dreams.

Realize that your collective Posts and Exchanges, whether you realize it or not, become your PERSONAL BRAND and SOCIAL MEDIA RESUME! Every single thing you post absolutely reflects your principles and values (or lack thereof). Always **fact check**, **grammar check** and **spell check** before you share.

To be effective, Engage in Conversational Intelligence: Judith Glaser, author of **"Conversational Intelligence"** said that conversational intelligence capability is hardwired into our DNA. Research is discovering that this begins to develop even as early as in the womb. The goal of conversational intelligence, among others is to be "WE-CENTRIC" as opposed to "I-CENTRIC" i.e. Openness, sharing, intentions, aspirations, respect, rapport, bonding with others and movement toward establishing common and aligned objectives. Scientific research has likewise validated that our brain's neuro-circuitry literally allows our brain to have a "cortisol bath" when we are "In TRUST" with another person. This holds true for social media communication! This is consistent with the principles of **synergistic interdependence** taught by Stephen Covey in the "7 Habits of Highly Effective People".

Understand that social media is a global mass communications network. Although the American constitution guarantees Freedom of Speech, the internet has shattered barriers in ways that previously were unheard of. It has built bridges towards better understanding as much as created a terrifying means for evil and wickedness to be perpetuated. Due to the tremendous diversity of people, what we [Americans] may "think" is *appropriate* may be deemed uncouth, ignorant, or worse prejudicial by other cultures (even our own). Post wisely. If you are a business entrepreneur, it is even more essential to check and re-check what we post on social media. Always ask yourself the following questions: What is my intention in sharing this post? Will it result in a positive response? Am I trying to provoke a dialogue or an argument? Am I being willfully obtuse and ignoring the underlying implications of my post?

The adage ***"do not share your dirty laundry in public"*** is a wise and useful principle to follow.

Transparency and Integrity in Relationships: It is of utmost importance to be mindful of the content we share, because everything that is seen on social media impacts someone's life - for good or for bad. If you are a professional or businessperson and want to use social media effectively, it is essential to own the responsibility for what you post. It is essential that the information you share is consistent with the "brand" you are developing. Ideally, your posts should reflect yours and your business's mission and core values. The seconds and minutes of time your followers and viewers invest in your post is extremely valuable to you!

If you are endorsing and advertising a product or service, for example, make sure you have had personal positive experience with it. If you have not, send the person or entity asking you to "Like" their page and let them know your thoughts – **be firm but be diplomatic and courteous**. For example, simply send a short note to say, "Thank you, but I am not interested at this time".

Respecting Yours and Other's Privacy: Depending on your goal - whether just to reach out to relatives and friends, or a full-on social media exposure to establish your Brand, you need to be considerate and respectful of other people's sensibilities. Adjust your PRIVACY SETTINGS accordingly. Pro-actively "MUTE" for content you do not need and "BLOCK" and "REPORT" entities you think are predatory or harmful.

LAST BUT NOT LEAST...

Emojis are fine, but humans love elegant words and images. Share TRUTH, BEAUTY, AND INSPIRATION - the power is at the end of your pretty fingertips!

CHAPTER 8

THE VERIDIVA NARRATIVE

Mercedita Noland

Like the diamond – my birthstone – my life is akin to this rough black rock. Mined from out of the darkness, brought into the light and honed to a fine brilliance. Like a beautifully cut and priceless diamond, I have many facets. I am strong when it matters and share my brilliance with those who choose to see it.

There are a million stories, anecdotes, and narratives inside of me. So many that I often feel I will burst until these stories have been told. Having come from a long line of strong women, I had to go through the journey of acceptance, and of embracing my own strengths – and to acknowledge the gifts that are innate in all of us. I had to close my ears to the noise that has been the constant tyrant in a life surrounded by many tyrants – those from without and even more sinister – those from within.

I realize, however, that for my voice to be heard and for my lessons to be shared, I have to begin from a place where other women can hear me – where nothing matters but the light, the purity, and the truth - that place is my soul. This is the story of VeriDiva – the seed, the motivation, the passion, the impetus, the journey, the brand, and the legacy.

I was named after my great maternal grandmother, Mercedes – hence Mercedita, which means "little Mercedes". Dona Mercedes was the epitome of unapologetic, feminine strength. She was also beautiful, gracious, forthright, and graceful. Her personal exploits alone would fill several volumes but suffice to say that she was a towering matriarch in my childhood and an indelible influence in my psyche. Our personalities - indeed our characters - are greatly shaped by the personalities and characters of those who have raised and nurtured us.

In the early sixties, my parents enrolled me in a private Catholic girl's school close to our home. Attending a private school for girls was everything that is cliché – along with receiving a great education - it was exclusive, expensive and most of the students were rich, spoiled little girls, doted upon by their parents, grandparents and often, their full-time governesses. I was an exception – my family though comfortable was not considered rich, but my parents believed in providing us with the best education they could afford. I was also doted upon by my parents, aunts, and grandparents, but hardly spoiled. I was an extremely intelligent and precocious child and I excelled academically without trying. I say this without any false modesty because, I experienced alienation early on in my childhood. I was smart and talented and because I was all those things, some of my classmates were extremely mean to me. They dis-included me in play activities at recess, lunchtime, and other group activities. To a sensitive girl – this is the cruelest form of bullying. ***It also planted the seed of a deep yearning to belong.***

I would go home and cry and ask Mercedes (and a slew of Aunts and Great Aunts) why my classmates were so mean to me. Mercedes, in her wisdom, did not coddle me, offer empty solace, nor justify the actions of the bullies. Herein lay the parable of the big, fat, and fruitful mango tree. For those who have seen a fruitful mango tree, you will notice that those golden juicy fruits hang in "clusters" from a branch.

Many childhood summers, my cousins and I were shipped by our parents to vacation in the province of Iloilo - my maternal clan's ancestral estate. There, we spent the entire season in idyllic days of playing, eating delicious food, attending fiestas, getting to know the locals, and participating in traditional summer activities such as the *"Flores de Mayo"* and the *"Santacruzan"*.

One day, Mercedes took me to the family orchard and said, "Do you see those little boys with the *tiradors* (home-made slingshots)"? "Notice how they only hit the big mango trees with lot of fruits"? "Notice too, how they don't bother with the trees that have little or no fruits"? "You, my dearest, are the big fat mango tree". "You will always take a hit, because people will always want what you have and what they aim to have". Mercedes taught me how to "fight the fight of the strong" – to never accept other people's cruelty as a reflection of who I am, but to look deep inside of me to see and understand why they do those things.

She taught me the art of just being present in the moment – long before "new age philosophy" made it a fashionable. Mercedes would often ask me to sit next to her and say in the sweetest way, *"Inday, patawhay"*. Roughly translated from the Ilongo dialect means, *"My dearest girl, just sit and relax and breathe"*.

Mercedes also taught me the art of compassion. Summers when my cousins and I would vacation in the province, she would take me to visit the poorer neighborhoods in the village. We would bring baskets of fresh mangoes, rice cakes and other items that she knew certain families needed. She had a way with them that they accepted her gifts without feeling like they were being judged or condescended upon. This experience, more than anything else unfailingly, reminds me how blessed we are to have been given so much.

Fast forward to the present. After having had successful careers in Manila and soon after college, I eventually immigrated to the United States. I met a charming and handsome man, fell in love, got married, had a child, and after 7 years, got divorced. Having successfully raised a child as a single mother, I realized that there are latent dreams I must yet fulfill. One of these dreams is **the idea and the ideal** of being with other women who are kindred spirits – women who shared the same idealism, optimism, compassion, and joyfulness of spirit that I experienced, learned from Mercedes and other mentors and profoundly internalized. I realized then as I do now, that this is quite a "tall order".

In 1996, the company where I started as a financial advisor selected their top producers who they dubbed as "studs" to become licensed facilitators (facilitating is a euphemism for innovative, interactive teaching) of the "7 Habits of Highly Effective People" (the book and the program), under the tutelage of Stephen Covey and company. I was one of those "studs" and had the great fortune to be trained by the best. As a facilitator, I became a dedicated disciple and practitioner of the universal principles taught within that book - the 7 Habits. At the core of the 7 Habits is the principle of "transformational relationships". It is based on the premise that our lives become exponentially better when we treat people in our lives as important and significant, where our actions are underlined by consideration and respect for others and beyond these considerations is to develop the habit of "seeking to understand others first before we seek to be understood."

My personal transformation is one of the hardest projects I have undertaken; and to be perfectly honest, I am still very much a work-in-progress. Over two decades of working as my own boss, and having a successful practice as a financial advisor, coalesced into a great body of knowledge that I fully realized can be taught and duplicated for the success of other women. In my work as a financial advisor, I have witnessed countless instances in which my highly successful women clients struggled with the realities of career and financial success, finding balance, and keeping their relationships, re-directing their energies and resources when they no longer feel fulfilled in their jobs, I created a path to enable them to achieve their own visions. To these women, I have become not simply a trusted professional partner, but also a mentor, coach, confidant, soul-sister, and most importantly -

friend. I have become part of their "invisible super-power team". In this arena, I *reign supreme*, because with the high level of trust and confidence put upon me by my clients, I had to be like "Caesar's wife" and be above reproach. My client's trust and confidence are a sacred silent contract.

One of the most demanding aspects of being a financial advisor is to consistently generate quality client-prospects. This profession is both social and insular. The end-result of what we do is long-term financial success for every single one of our clients. Within that world, however, is a profound level of isolation because advisors must protect their clients' privacy at all costs, precisely because of the inherent trust they have conferred on us. In other words, information we have about our clients may not be shared even with those closest to us. The paradox is that we must network heavily to meet and develop those quality client-prospects.

Decades of networking and serving in leadership positions with various organizations opened my eyes to the different ways people connect with each other. It also opened my eyes to the deficiencies of "old school" clique-ish ways of networking and the old dream came back to the surface.

In 2010, I founded VeriDiva Women's Business Networking Group. Its core values are based on the principles of "transformational relationship" networking model. In October 2020, we will be celebrating 10 years of this magnificent sisterhood – an ideal that is now a reality for dozens of women-entrepreneurs -that continues to grow. The dream is alive and ever evolving and we owe it all to my Great Grandmother Mercedes.

CHAPTER 9

MY ADVENTURE WITH FOOD

Mercedita Noland

I was born and raised in the Philippines - a country with a rich cultural heritage and an even richer near-adoration of food. It is an agricultural country - rice and fish - were the staple diet, and therefore, everything that comes from the Earth and the Sea are held sacred and as precious as breath. My culture - religious inclinations notwithstanding - holds the belief that a lot of food is the equivalent to Heavenly blessings, and therefore a lot of food equals abundance and prosperity. We are also a culture of unparalleled generosity and hospitality. Every important life event is marked by a tremendous amount of food.

This is the story of my relationship with food. To understand my cultural history is to understand my pervasive and ubiquitous search for the perfect balance in my personal nourishment – both body and soul. Food is powerful and one of the defining aspects of our physical health and well-being. I am a "Foodie"! It is significant to note that **Filipino Cuisine** is a glorious amalgamation of the Malay, Chinese, Spanish, and American cultural and gustatory influences. Most of our recipes have been adjusted to reflect a certain taste using indigenous ingredients, while respecting the original influences and many have retained their Spanish and Chinese names, for example, *arroz valenciana, paella, mechado, empanada, chop suey* and *siopao.*

My family - from both the unit and the broader perspective - is a mixture of abundance and scarcity. On my maternal side, we held great value in education and culture, and on the paternal side, we held great value in business and the expansion of family wealth. We also have aspects of great dysfunction where a branch is "cut-off" – many for reasons based on antiquated Victorian values that were a legacy of nearly four hundred years of Spanish conquest and, those who were cut-off therefore, experienced poverty and scarcity. Nearly four hundred years where our original Malay culture was ruthlessly sublimated in the name of Christianity and the sovereigns of Spain. To know this is to understand – a lot!

In my childhood, there is a strict adherence to meals at the family table, and a tacit understanding that one has to "eat everything that's on one's plate". One, therefore, does not overfill one's plate and leave food. You can get as much as you want, go for seconds and thirds, but anything you put on your plate must be consumed. Family meals were strict and absolute appointments, and one is only excused if one was at work, in school or bed-ridden by an illness. It is a sign of one's fine upbringing and good manners when one is a guest and eats everything on the plate.

As a young and skinny girl, I was very picky and did not like to eat much, and did not have an appetite, particularly in the mornings. When I started kindergarten, my mother went on an irrational campaign to "fatten me up" and there were countless mornings when I was literally forced to eat toast, eggs, bacon or sausage and milk. I would usually eat only the toast and bacon. When I do not eat, there would be great strife and drama - from my mother, who believes that I will develop "stomach ulcers" if I do not eat *a lot of food*. Some days, the maids would "pack a lunch" for school - which oftentimes I did not eat because the food became cold, greasy, and unappetizing. Sometimes, my parents would pay expensively to the private school so I could eat a hot meal in the lunch hall, or my Mom or my Aunts would bring a "fresh-cooked meal" to school during lunch and bribe me with Fruitella candy to "finish everything that was prepared". In the "lunch hall", I did not eat much either because sometimes I did not like the food, often I got involved in conversations with classmates such that I neglected to eat. In all three scenarios, I fared best with the Mom and Aunts bringing fresh-cooked lunch (along with the candy bribe).

In 3rd grade, my parents enrolled me at a Private Catholic Boarding School. There were wonderful nuns at that school, but I hated the food and hated the schedule even more. We had to wake up at 5 am to attend mass, then back to the dormitory to shower and change at 6 am, breakfast at 7 am and school at 8 am. I did not eat breakfast. I went to school hungry and promptly fell asleep by the third period. Although I was a brilliant student, I could not keep up with most of the class, because I was so sleep and nutritionally deprived. The nuns had to call my parents to let them know I was not going to survive there and recommended that I transfer to a different school as an extern. After a semester, my parents enrolled me in a "public school" closer to home. This meant a whole lot more freedom and less regimentation. I ate better and made lots of friends.

Summers were wonderful! My family loved to travel - we went on many, many excursions, day trips to different "beauty spots" such as Lake Taal (Taal Volcano), Pagsanjan Falls, and Los Banos and had extended vacations in the Summer Capital (Baguio City in the Mountain Province) or in Iloilo. These trips presented gustatory experiences that I associate with happy memories.

Summer vacations in Iloilo which is my maternal grandparents home province in the Visayan Islands was always a blast. Here, I participated in many beautiful customs of my Great Grandmother, Great Aunts, Great-great aunts, and dozens of cousins. I was somehow related to everyone up to the third and 4th degrees. I went to the annual *"Flores de Mayo"* which was a month-long daily dedication of flowers to the Blessed Virgin Mary. In the mornings, my best friend Gracia and I would walk for many miles, go to the different neighborhoods, gather flowers from both private & public gardens, go home, pull them apart and place the petals in home-crafted "tin baskets" decorated with white curled Japanese paper (which we made ourselves). Our hands always smelt like a garden! In the afternoon, we attended the special church services where all the girls walked down the church aisles, end-to-front, to the main altar, while throwing flower petals to honor Mary. The last day of May is the *Grand Gala* event where the town's beauty queens are paraded in cars festooned with flowers and all manners of glitter - this is major *"fiesta"* time!

A *"Fiesta"* is a traditional town feast where every home is an "open house", and every town folk is involved in the preparation of days-long feasting, drinking, dancing, and pageantry. It is a celebration of thanks for the bountiful harvest and an excuse to socialize on a grand scale. Every home in every town was a veritable "open house". My Aunts and cousins and I went in and out of many friends' and relatives' homes to visit, bring food, eat food, and celebrate. I partook in all the festivities. I made lots of friends, sang, danced & ate. I was never sick when on vacation - I ate well as a natural part of everyday life (without being coerced), I never over-ate nor over-indulged and I was always glowing with good health! Everything was planted, harvested, milled, churned, and cooked by everyone.

Everything was from the earth and the sea - the rice, the fruits and vegetables, the beef, the pork, the chicken, the fish, shells, and oysters and even the herbs and seasonings. Everything was made from fresh ingredients and many of the fruits and vegetables came straight from either our own or a relative's farm and/or kitchen. There was no processed food, even the ice cream was hand-made straight from the family dairy and painstakingly churned with sea salt! ***I have to say this one of the most serene and happy seasons of my childhood!***

Back in Manila and throughout most of the summer, meals ended with fresh, golden, sweet Manila champagne mangoes! I used to think of this as ***"mango orgy"***. The tenant-farmers would deliver bushels of this delicious fruit and we would enjoy it every day until it was gone! My mother and I would call a truce, because many of the dishes served were my favorites and there was no question - I ate well.

Every birthday, christening, wedding, and death anniversaries was an excuse to have a family fiesta. We would have **lechon** - the ultimate centerpiece for any Filipino gathering worth its name! **Lechon** is a whole pig, butchered, gutted, ran through with a bamboo pole, and roasted over spit charcoal for long hours. The skin is golden brown, buttery crisp, and the meat is moist, juicy, and tender! The food constantly abounds - all the other entrees of vegetables, fresh salads, all manner of delicacy - take supporting roles to the lechon

Except for the desserts. Oh the desserts! Because rice is our main grain staple, there are numerous sweets made with rice flour - *bibingka, puto, kuchinta, sapin-sapin, maja-blanca, biko, suman & palitaw to name a few.* These were either baked or steamed and most are garnished with fresh coconut cream and raw brown sugar called "panutsa" ground & sifted from its original half-ball shape; many are served with fresh-shaven mature coconut flakes or drizzled with coconut caramel made fresh with raw brown sugar. There are also *leche-flan, macapuno, fruita de crema, braso de Mercedes and cassava cake (made with cassava flour*. These were just the traditional desserts. Our Chinese-Filipino friends and relatives would bring *"tikoy"*, moon cakes and *"hopia" (layered pastry with sweet bean pastes)* during Chinese New Year.

As I got older, my tastes and food culture became more diverse when I went to work and as my social circle grew. I was introduced to authentic Thai, Italian, French, German, Cuban, Mediterranean and Japanese cuisines. I began to travel, and my travel further enhanced my foodie adventure.

After I emigrated to the United States, I assimilated into the American culture by learning to eat American fare – burgers and fries, fried chicken and Mexican fast-food. Years later, I traveled to different cities and countries, and learned to appreciate each country's cuisine. I especially enjoy French cuisine ever since I visited Paris for the first time. I think this is because there is an obvious parallel to Filipino cuisine and cultural inclination – in how the French are obsessive about how their food is prepared from - freshest and finest ingredients. I enjoyed them all, but my heart, soul, and stomach have been irrevocably claimed by Filipino food – it represents to me comfort, joy, and home!

Finally, during this year of the COVID-19 Pandemic has made it universally challenging for all of us especially in terms of food and nourishment. Food is essential for life and wellbeing. Many segments of our society - school children, whose working parents rely on the school system to provide at least one full meal for their children during the school week, single mothers with infants and young children, the homebound elderly, the disabled living alone with no family support and the homeless relying on soup kitchens for meals, have been doubly hard-hit. It is heartening to know that charity, compassion, and social consciousness abound.

Many of us in the private, corporate sectors, and non-profit organizations have banded together to deliver food to those in need during the lockdowns and quarantine periods. I sincerely hope you find it in your hearts to reach out to help others. Contact your local churches, the Salvation Army, Feeding America, and even Walmart. Find out if your local restaurants have a food recycling program and see if you can assist in distributing meals even just around your neighborhood. There is so much we can do to alleviate hunger, and in doing so, in turn feed our souls.

ABOUT THE AUTHOR

Mercedita Noland

Mercedita Noland or *Mercy* as her intimates call her is the quintessential dreamer, stargazer, and perpetual romantic. As highly analytical and left-brained as she can be, especially in her main work, she invariably chooses to read and travel more than any other activity. In books she finds the mental and emotional reprieve from a very demanding and exacting career. In her travels, she gets the validation of her hard work by expanding her horizons, discovering beautiful and exotic destinations, and learning about other cultures.

Mercy is a seasoned career registered financial professional who has been serving clients since 1996. As of this publication, she is a Financial Advisor with a major

U.S. Broker Dealer and Registered Investment Advisor. Based in Temecula Valley, Mercy is a highly trained Specialist who is dedicated to helping her clients define and achieve their financial goals. She takes a holistic, total-needs and long-term approach as a formula for success. Her track record is exemplified by high client retention and trans-generational wealth transfer. She is also Founder and C.E.O. of VeriDiva Women's Business Networking Group.

As a passionate lifetime advocate for women and children, she is actively involved in various local and global charities and not-for-profit organizations. Her primary charity - Smile Train – a children's charity that provides free cleft repair surgeries to underserved children in more than 88 of the world's developing countries. She has received numerous awards both for her work as a Financial Advisor, Civic Leader and Women and Children's Advocacy.

Mercy added the title "Author" to her resume in 2019 and 2020 by having her first short non-fiction narratives published in 2 anthologies. This book – "Diamonds of Wisdom" - is a culmination of her dream to produce her own anthology along with sister-friends.

Mercy is an avid world traveler and counts Paris as the "city of her soul". When she is not working with clients, coaching other women entrepreneurs, reading (always reading), or travelling, she spends leisure time with her fiancé Rod and their adorable puppy, Jean Luc.

CHAPTER 10

LETTER TO MY YOUNGER SELF

Annabelle Troin

My dearest friend, Isik, who is like a father to me, asked me the following question on my 60th birthday: "Are you happy how your life has turned out?"

This question threw me off a little as he did not say "satisfied", "fulfilled" or "regretful" …. he asked if I am happy. I realized that I had never seriously asked myself this question. Life just happened and while I made decisions to go in certain directions, I never had an overall view of what my life should be like.

As the universe would have it, while on a weekend hike the song "Dear Younger Me" played on my iPhone. As I listened to the following lyrics of the song, I started to cry.

> *Dear younger me*
> *I cannot decide*
> *Do I give some speech about how to get*
> *the most out of your life?*

Or do I go deep
And try to change
The choices that you'll make 'because
they're choices that made me?
Even though I love this crazy life,
Sometimes I wish it were a smoother ride.

I recall my dear friend asking me the question and it had me wondering what I actually had learned from this life. So I embarked upon writing my own little "Letter to My Younger Self". As it turns out, I learned quite a lot when life just happened. Some lessons may be more obvious than others. So here is my letter to my younger self ….

Dear Bee,

I know you will not appreciate me calling you that since you never liked the nickname "Bee" … but this is how I think of you, my younger self. You also did not like your name "Annabelle" and even asked Mom if you could change your name to Veronica. I am glad you stayed with your given name "Annabelle".

You are 16 right now. I am 60 years old. I am writing this letter to you on our 60th birthday to simply impart what I have learned in this journey of life. That said, take what is useful from this advice and leave behind what is not. I know you are not going to take much notice of what

I am writing. You do not like receiving guidance from adults. This is a trait that is going to stay with you, I am afraid.

So here goes…

First of all, I am so proud of you for leaving a "destructive" home environment at 18-years-old and putting your dreams and goals ahead of everything else. I know that you will be scared and wonder whether it was all a mistake. This will be the very first lesson in following your intuition. That fear will be overcome by confidence. You will work, as hard as you never have before, to be able to fulfill your goals. It will not be easy. You will work and go to school part-time.

It will take you more than six years to get your Mechanical Engineering Degree. But it will be worth it.

At some point you will be able to acknowledge that it was quite courageous what you did – leaving everything behind and following your dream. This is when you will have necessary distance and clarity. Hindsight is a beautiful thing.

This is the first time you have gone after something you really feel passionate about -- and to accept and understand why people act the way they do. As it turns out, you were wise not to think too much about things in advance. Otherwise, you would have been frozen in fear.

Where purpose, passion and skill collide, bliss resides. Do not worry about trying to know what path or career you want to choose – take college seriously, it is the door that will open opportunities for you. Just be open, try everything, always be curious, continue to learn and listen to how you feel. Purpose, Passion, Skill...put them all together. Your passions and career choices will change so do not get too comfy.

When your first love breaks your heart, it will feel like the end of the world, but I assure you, it is not, it is the beginning. You will pick yourself back up and meet life-long friends you would not have met without that breakup, so let him go. One day you will understand why it was not meant to work out, but for now, do not blame yourself, because you are and always will be good enough.

You will find that one person who will love you for who you are. He will bring out the best in you and challenge you to be independent. He will teach you how to rotate the tires on your car; show you the difference between vice-grip locking pliers and tongue-and-groove pliers; take you out on a small boat regatta knowing well you cannot swim; take you car-racing and show you how to take the apex of a turn. He will teach you to love unconditionally and he will leave to teach you to trust your own decisions again.

His death will turn your world upside down. His sudden death will bring out guilt, blame and a lot of pain and sorrow. It will take you years to accept that "death" is God's way of bringing something new. Something must end in order to start something new. His death does not mean you have failed, because there is no such thing as failure. It is all part of your process, so trust it.

You will eventually begin to understand why certain things did not work out, and why certain people do not stick around. You will start to see that all of the miniature disasters you go through are the universe's way of keeping you on your path, and them on theirs, even if it is not what you want in that moment.

You will have times when you will doubt yourself. You will analyze the way you look, act, and think. It will be hard but try to believe in who you are and the decisions you have made, because you are a smart, kind, generous and beautiful girl.

Try to practice understanding, how to let things be as they are, and not how you think they should be, because this will be a necessity in your career, in your relationships, and in your life.

Learn to push your own buttons.

Inspire yourself. Everyone else is busy. It is wonderful

and convenient when others inspire us but there will be droughts between the supply and demand. Make peace with being alone; no need to look for better company than yourself ……. Use your alone time to pamper yourself, 'because you deserve nothing less.

This is how we make inspiration sustainable and scalable. Learn to meditate … love the stillness and quietness of silence. It is in silence that we hear God speak to us. Our strongest source of inspiration is nature — being outdoors. It will be our church where we can commune with God (the Universe). Close your eyes. Breathe deeply. Smile.

Do not let other people rent space in your head for free. Guard your most personal & most valuable real estate. What other people think of you is none of your business. Be you and let go. Repeat. This is a tough one for us. It requires constant practice. We struggle and trip over this one at times. Learn to forgive quickly, but do not let anyone walk all over you. Stand up for yourself. Stand up for what you believe. Believe that there is goodness in this world and make it your life's mission to seek out and find this goodness.

Read. Read. Read. Make it a part of your day, your world. Be a constant learner; challenge your own opinions. You will be a student for the rest of your life so never stop learning new things. The best part is that you get to learn things you are interested in, explore and the best part is that grades do not matter anymore. Be a sponge for knowledge and learn how to enjoy the learning process.

Travel. Even if it is just an hour from where you live. Exploring will open your mind. If you have an opportunity to travel due to your career, take the ticket and explore while working — especially while you are young and have less geographic anchors. Do not wait for a travel buddy ... explore on your own.

Make exercise a priority. It was never very high on our list to do, it all seemed too intense. Our weight will go through all the fluctuations over the years, but we discovered hiking and got ourselves outdoors. Then we got introduced to tango dancing and rediscovered our love for dancing. So we learned to appreciate the power of exercise for both physical and mental health.

Words matter. With all relationships, exchange "we" vs. "me" as much as possible.

Try not to worry so much about these: your career, your weight, your finances, your future, etc. It all works out. I know this is one of our weaknesses ... but always remember that we are warriors, not worriers. Your career is going to take off. You will be successful, but please do not let your career become a priority over family.

You will distance yourself from Mom...afraid of repeating history all over again. But you will learn that it is through you that she got to live her own dreams. She was as happy as a bride on your wedding day; she was so proud wearing your cap as you received your Master's Degree; she eagerly landscaped your backyard with beautiful pink roses (because she knows you love roses) when you bought your first home; and held you close as you cried to sleep after Peter's death.

In her last days, you will become her caretaker. You will finally hear those words you have been aching to hear all your life: "I love you and thank you." In her last few months, you will finally see Mom for the woman she is (was). You will finally understand why she made the choices she made and forgive her ….and forgive yourself.

The answer to "why" which you so desperately searched for during that time will not come. It cannot come. Not every question has an answer. But something amazing will come out of all of this, as you will rediscover what you are passionate about and you will finally reconnect your head to your heart.

You will lose people (husband, mother, nephew, in-laws) in a matter of eight years. And when you thought you were planning the last years of your career before retirement, you will lose your job. You will use this to build something new. You will build yourself back with a purpose that truly transfixes you. You will still be scared, but much less so, as you have learned so much on your way.

Getting comfortable with being uncomfortable is extremely powerful. It takes daily practice. Push yourself to take calculated risks. When in doubt, ask yourself: What is the worst thing that could happen if I try ____? And then what? Will ____ make me happy? How will _____ benefit me in pursuit of my ____ goals?

Learn when to make things happen versus when to let things happen. If you are torn on whether to let something happen or make it happen then sit down or take a hike …. slow down, be still, and listen to your inner voice. Our personality drives us to make things happen (force it) at times. Learn to pause and listen to your instincts. Timing is everything. Trust that things happen for us and not to us.

You have been through a lot already, but because of it all, you will know to stand up for what you believe in, even if it means standing alone. Learn to love your own company. Laugh at your mistakes and celebrate your victories.

And most of all, be grateful for all you have. Never take for granted all the blessings in your life …. Even the disappointments and heartache are blessings because you grow stronger and wiser in the difficult times. Be grateful for all you have been given. At the end of the day, be grateful for all the blessings of the day and be mindful that today is all you are promised. And be a blessing to all those around you.

I am so proud of you.

ABOUT THE AUTHOR

Annabelle Troin

Annabelle Troin, or "AB" to close friends and family, was born and raised in the Philippines. Her dad named her Annabelle after his favorite poem from Edgar Allan Poe "Annabel Lee."

It was many and many a year ago,
In a kingdom by the sea,
That a maiden there lived whom you may know
By the name of Annabel Lee;
And this maiden she lived with no other thought
Than to love and be loved by me.

As the middle child and the only girl in a family of four, she grew up a tomboy. Her family taught her to be independent, self-reliant and claim her place in the world. They are the first people who taught her to be accountable, challenged her to be comfortable with the uncomfortable and in turn set the example on how to do it. To pay it forward, Annabelle has started a "Math Lab" program at the Catholic School in her community church to help young boys and girls realize that it does not matter where you come from, what you look like, what society deems you to be, or the like. The program brings in professionals in the community to volunteer their time and talent to tutor in math and science, as well as encourage their mentees to know their value, profit off their talents, and surround themselves with people who appreciate them. Given the opportunity to help someone … just do it.

Annabelle holds both a Mechanical Engineering Degree from California Polytechnic University, Pomona and a master's degree in Accounting and Finance from University of California, Irvine. She has diverse experience in process engineering, environmental law, banking, and finance. Annabelle spent her early career as an engineer working for various engineering consulting firms and the oil/gas industry. Upon completion of her MBA, Annabelle launched her second career in banking and finance. She is currently employed by one of the top 10 banks in the world and focuses on regulatory compliance, system engineering and process development.

Annabelle has also been highly active in the Filipino Community in Long Beach and is currently serving as President of the Filipino Ministry for Our Lady of Refuge Church. The Ministry is focused on promoting Filipino culture in the Archdiocese of Los Angeles, provides support to Catholic Charities in educational tutoring and mentoring and liaises with local Filipino businesses to assist local charities – the Ministry Group was instrumental in providing much needed food and supplies to parish priests in the community during the COVID-19 pandemic quarantine. Annabelle has also been an active volunteer for Feed America – and has helped distribute food to elderly seniors during the pandemic.

She is also a member of the National Alliance for Global Leadership (NAGL) at her company. One of NAGL's primary goals is to promote and elevate women in executive leadership through mentorship and coaching.

Annabelle has recently rediscovered her love for dancing and has been taking Tango lessons. Hiking has been her passion as of late, even her little Shih Tzu puppy "Mila" has taken to it as well. She is also an avid traveler and looking forward to another trip to Paris.

CHAPTER 11

THE PINK BUBBLE

Sandie Fuenty

Years ago if you had ever told me that I would be in direct sales, I would have told you, "Never, you are nuts." Never say never.

My journey has some high points and some low points. The lesson of my story is to never give up.

After graduating from high school, I held several secretarial and executive assistant positions for insurance companies and the executives/owners of the Northern Trust Bank, a long-standing family-owned landmark in downtown Chicago. I also ran a service bureau at night, when IBM punch cards and huge mainframes were in existence. I learned to do just about anything to survive.

In the early 80's my husband, our 2-year-old son and I moved to California. Jim had come out to California to check out a business opportunity and fell in love with Southern California. The weather was much different than the hots and colds we experienced in the Midwest and had grown up with. A partnership was formed between him and a friend and they sold and installed front-end alignment equipment. While this was going on, I was back in Illinois dealing with selling a house in a down market, raising a little one by myself and working.

We were leaving family, friends, work, a house we owned for the unknown. I felt like the pioneers must have. (My ancestors journeyed in covered wagons and settled in the southern area of Illinois in Edgar County.) Our son and I flew out with several suitcases and several boxes on the plane and left Illinois behind.

Once we got to California, I was so happy to see my husband again (for almost a year we had been long distance). We moved into an apartment paying more than our house payments had been. Oh, did I mention that after 8 months we finally sold the house at breakeven? There was no profit to bring out to California. Three months after we uprooted ourselves and came to the land of milk and honey, Jim's partner absconded with the money from the business. This was such a bittersweet start for our new life. I was able to find a job doing administrative subjects, Jim picked up whatever work he could find and learned expertise in heating and air-conditioning and we were able to put Jimmy in preschool part-time. Life was not easy, but there was love.

I have a baby sister (4 years younger than me) that I left in Illinois along with my mom and dad. We are very tuned into each other. Soon after we moved to California, Deb called me to tell me about this great new product she had just tried and, lo and behold, I told her how I had just been to a Mary Kay party a couple of days before. We laughed at how our experiences were so similar, almost 2000 miles apart. We get to see each other once a year for the family reunion and it is like no time has passed. We just pick right up from where we left off (we talk on average once a week) and go shopping together and laugh at our changing bodies before I go home. It is our special time together each year and eagerly awaited. We had to miss it this year but one way or another we will get together soon.

My neighbors at the apartment complex knocked on our door and invited me to come to a party they were having with makeup and stuff. That is when I was introduced to Mary Kay, the products, the Company, and the foundation of the Company. After doing the facial I came home and asked my husband what he thought, and I will never forget his words. "Get it". "It looks better than what you've been wearing". He is a man of few words and always has been and always will be. That meant he liked it and it looked great.

What brought me into the Company? First, I needed something fun to do and to make money in my spare time. Second, I resonated with the priorities of Mary Kay Ash. She believed that as women, if we kept our priorities as Faith first, Family second, Career third, we could be successful and not have to sacrifice our children to get there. And, lastly, the company believed in the Golden Rule – to treat others as we wanted to be treated. From experience I knew that Corporate America was not like that.

Mary Kay was my Plan B during my J.O.B.s (Just Over Broke), while running my husband's A/C business, during my surgery when I was off work for 5 months. And my little hobby kept bringing me money from reorders and my middle school daughter's advertising. I considered my Mary Kay to be my fun and my sanity, since I was mostly working around men in construction. I would be out on a job with Jim, with my good clothes hanging in the truck, and on meeting night, as we were driving back to Orange County from wherever we were working, you would see this lady putting on her makeup, fluffing up her hair, and changing into her blouse, skirt, jacket, panty hose and pumps. I got really good at changing and never worried about it unless we were next to a big rig. Then I would stop for decency's sake to make sure I did not shock that driver.

We came to California with Jimmy in 1980. Jimmy as a child never met a stranger. He would talk with anyone from the time he could walk and talk. During his school years, his major chore was yard work, and he would do it each Saturday morning. It was amazing how the girls from his school always seemed to walk by during his mowing time. His biggest rebellious act was to climb out his bedroom window at night so his best friend Daniel could pick him up and teach him to drive stick-shift. Why? Because our pastor told him that he could use his red Corvette to go to Prom if he knew how to drive stick. So Jimmy learned and drove his date to Prom in a Corvette. He never tried drugs or smoked.

Our daughter, Lindsey, on the other hand, tested us constantly. She was quiet, strong willed. When she started high school, her life changed, and she became part of a new group of friends that led to trial after trial. This ranged from being a runaway for almost the entire summer between sophomore and junior year, to having a relationship with a heroin addict, experimenting with drugs and alcohol, and going to a remedial school for half of junior year. There she met the principal Mr. Marzelli who realized she was not a discipline problem but just needed to be useful, and he changed her direction. She went back to regular high school for Senior year and we were scared until we heard that they had a new principal. It was Mr. Marzelli and he communicated with her all during that year and when she graduated, he handed her HER diploma, and gave her a hug.

In 1983 my husband formed Precision Air and became an independent heating and a/c contractor. All this happened as I was on bed rest waiting the eventual birth of our daughter. Jimmy showed up a month early and Lindsey appeared almost 3 weeks late in a matter of 2 ½ hours.

I had had a miscarriage before each healthy child, so we all agreed that if she was healthy, she was the last. Personalities are so different in children, even from birth. Hers was evident at about 4 years old, when she very seriously told me, "Mom, you know I have to learn how to do things by myself". "You trying to tell me how to do it so that I don't get hurt, isn't going to work". Boy, did she know what she was talking about and what we would find out during the years to come. Our son was exceptionally smooth and even; our daughter was a roller coaster ride.

My Mary Kay has allowed this shy little girl who never followed any dreams (except following her husband to California) to flap her wings. I was raised in an era when most girls were raised to finish high school, get a job (secretarial or airline stewardess or teacher), until we got married and had children. Careers and achievement were not considered proper when I was growing up.

I have enjoyed my Mary Kay business, achieving different levels of success, earning money, and moving up. I have earned the use of 5 Company cars over my 27 years in Mary Kay. I have been big, I have been little, and everything in between, but I have never left the Company. I grew so much personally and was honored to be asked to speak at an annual Southern California event (Jamboree) in front of 1500 attendees. I was never a loud person seeking attention. I was soft spoken, took direction from my bosses, I had strong work ethics, worked hard. But there was always **a rebel inside of me wanting to break out**. Training in Mary Kay also taught me essential business acumen so that I was able to hold my own in the construction industry and be able to go face to face with project managers, owners, and stand my ground and voice my opinion, even though I was the only lady in the room. My Mary Kay colleagues described me as a "breath of fresh air" when I walked into a room.

In 1996 I underwent surgery for pre-cancerous severe ulcerative colitis after dealing with the disease and medications for over 8 years. The steroids were the worst part. Prednisone caused me to gain almost 70 pounds, creating cataracts and fatty deposits throughout my body. My mom got off an airplane and walked right past me because she did not recognize me. I did not recognize me! My colon was removed, and I had an ileostomy bag for several months till I was healthy enough to have the second surgery to remove the bag. I was off work for a total of five months. During the time I was laid up, my Mary Kay business kept working even though I could not. It opened my eyes to what was possible. What if I did put more effort into it? In February of 1998 I gave notice and my boss said, "Oh, Sandie, you know you'll have to go back to work for someone else so why don't you just reconsider and stay with us since we've invested time and money in you". I replied to him that I never planned to work for someone else again and I have not. Six months after resigning, I earned my first car and, of course, I drove up and took my friends at work to lunch to show it off, and one year later became a Director.

In 2001 my brother-in-law, Henryk, became ill with a brain tumor and within six months died. He had been in Vietnam about the same time as Jim and told Jim to make sure he went and did the Agent Orange Registry at the VA. Agent Orange was a pesticide that was sprayed to kill the foliage in Vietnam. Later it became obvious that it kills the people that touched or inhaled it also. We did and over the next 20 years we have watched this strapping, virile man's body slowly deteriorating. In 2014 we had to close his business due to his health. He suffers from uncontrollable diabetes, neuropathies of the arms and legs, gastroparesis, spinal stenosis, failing kidneys, and may be facing another back surgery to help him walk. This is not how we planned our twilight years to be.

In 2003 we moved to Lake Elsinore and bought our first house in California. Then the recession came, and we were forced to do a short sale after several years of working with the bank to do a loan modification. We were blessed to be able to find houses to rent in the same general area, until we could buy again. We started looking for houses to buy at the beginning of 2017. With the realtor and lender that I chose, we just were not making any progress. I notified them that if we were not in contract on a house by November, we would be going elsewhere. We did.

Everyone I talked to said we could not buy a new house because of the taxes, etc. We found a new real estate agent and the second house she took us to see was in a brand-new community. Before we drove in, I questioned her and said that we were told we could not buy new. She said she had passed this by her lender, and there was no reason we could not. We looked, fell in love, and bought with the VA Loan that Jim had never used. In the end of 2017 and early 2018, we watched OUR house be built and moved in on February 23, 2018. It is a perfect house for us and our aging experiences: single story, small backyard, perfect location, and amenities. Sophia, our granddaughter, has been able to make great use of the parks and swimming pools and splash park just a block or two away from our house.

In about 2016 I needed to get out and promote my business as a business. I went to network meetings and learned how to talk about myself and advertise my business. Oh, what a learning experience this was. But many of the different people I met became especially important in my life.

In early 2015, I was in the hospital and Jimmy, Sara and Lindsey drove out to visit and Jimmy and Sara were acting incredibly quiet, nervous, strange. They kept looking at this Thai cookbook they had purchased. Sara was born in Thailand. When visiting hours had come to an end, Jimmy handed me the Thai cookbook to look at and I noticed a photo in there that I thought someone had left in the book. Well it was an ultrasound showing us the beginnings of our little Sophia and it took us a few minutes to realize that this was them letting us know we were going to be grandparents. Finally, on December 12, 2015, Sophia was born, and we were able to be there for her birth. Not in the same room but right outside in the waiting room and we heard her first cry and knew she was ours.

We were notified that the rental house we were living in was being put on the market. Our son asked us to consider living with them for a couple months so we did not have to sign a lease and could save money and take care of an IRS issue. We thought about it and did. Little did we, or he, know that our daughter was going to move back in with us less than a month before we had to move out! So, 3 adults, 3 cats and 2 dogs moved into our son's house. It was 1500 square feet with one working bathroom, a total of 5 adults, 5 dogs and 3 cats, and our 2-year-old granddaughter. Love was tested during this time, but we all came out of it with laughter, grumbles, and a closeness that has lasted.

We grew into schedules that worked. Jimmy and Sara both worked outside of the house and had to be out by 7:30 am. I stayed in bed, out of their way, till the coast was clear. I then ran to the bathroom. It was not really running because it was right next to my room and I could hear everything. Lindsey's room was a closed in sun porch, so each time she had to go to the bathroom or come in the house, she had to go through my "bedroom". Lindsey worked a varied schedule and could also be flexible for bath and kitchen time.

Sophia went to her Grandmother's on Friday, her Grandfather's on Thursday, Jimmy had Mondays off, so we took care of Sophia and watched her grow on Tuesdays and Wednesdays. And we played "musical dogs" since most of the 5 had to be kept separated. After we moved into our new house, we would drive in one or two days a week, in the dark of the morning, and fight the traffic to spend the day with Sophia. We were both tired and took shifts and napped when she did. But there is such a closeness now, and before COVID-19 we would pick her up from pre-school and bring her home with us on Thursdays and take her home Friday night. Now we do not get to see her very often except via FaceTime and occasional pool days.

2020 arrived and the Pandemic hit. We were in our new house. I had to learn "virtual" and how to deal with social media, Zoom, Messenger, Facebook, etc. For a 70-year-old woman, this was and still is remarkably interesting and sometimes frustrating. Our 4 ½ year granddaughter can move around on my iPhone like it's no big deal. She can show me how to go onto many different apps and maneuver through them and I just sit there in awe. You need to remember that I learned to type on a manual typewriter where you pushed the keys down hard and pushed the return bar back to get to your next line of typing. I learned how to operate a mimeograph machine (with its obnoxious chemical smells), a comptometer (precursor to the adding machine), and eventually a word processor and a fax machine that had a roller that spun around with your document on it and transmitted the page through the phone lines.

But I learned to pivot and thrive with my business in the early months of 2020. In a period of 2 months my team and I built ourselves to be a Unit in Mary Kay with me as their Director (the top 2% of the Company). The following month of August we earned the use of a new 2021 Chevy Malibu which should be arriving before the end of November (I believe it will be here by my birthday on November 17). All this during a Pandemic... It has been so exhilarating watching this unfold, all the help and support I have received from friends, my clients, my unit, family. And they are so proud of me. At 70 years old (71 in November) this is quite an accomplishment for an "old" lady.

I do not "think" of myself as old – regardless of what it says on my driver's license - and I never will allow myself to stop living.

Lindsey and I were to have gone on a dream trip to Paris, France, in October of 2020, with the VeriDivas to celebrate their 10th Anniversary of its founding. Due to the Pandemic travel restriction we had to be postpone the trip until 2021. My VeriDiva sisters and I look forward to this event and joy of traveling and adventures. To celebrate and to ease the disappointment of not going to Paris, we took a trip to Las Vegas and had a celebratory dinner at the Eiffel Tower at The Paris Las Vegas Hotel. We envisioned being in the real Paris and enjoyed every minute of it.

While we were in Vegas, I received a call from Lindsey asking if I would consider going to Waco, TX with her for a retreat. The only issue was we would have to leave Sunday and I was returning from Vegas on Wednesday. She is a Bar Manager and Server at a Country Club and also started a business bringing furniture back to life and donating a portion of the proceeds to dog rescues. So all the bigwigs were going to be at this retreat and all of a sudden 2 tickets had become available. We went and I barely unpacked my suitcase. She made all the plans, found us an adorable little Airbnb; she was supposed to be there. She met all these women she was following on Facebook that owned the paint companies, were all artists in their own rights whether on furniture or canvas. She faced her fear and went up and helped paint in front of people and actually allowed herself to be vulnerable with these people. She has found her "tribe" and I approve. I am so blessed that our children want us in their lives.

What else do I do to occupy my time except for my husband and family? I am Secretary of the Board of Officers of VeriDiva Women's Business Networking Group – an elite women's business working group – that has for me become a treasured sisterhood. I am a Director for GSFE (Global Society for Female Entrepreneurs) Lake Elsinore/Murrieta/Wildomar Chapter and facilitate a monthly meeting. I am active at my church and, of course, I am now loving working my virtual Mary Kay business and meeting people all over the country through the magic of video conferencing – people I never would have been able to (or even thought of) prior to this Pandemic. I enjoy being a wife, mom, and Nana.

What has my Mary Kay business brought me? I have learned that I am worth it and have been rewarded with friends, cars, money, recognition, personal growth, enduring many trials, the joy of finding mentors and passing on mentorship, enriching other's lives, strength, great skin, travel and fun and watching dreams come true.

I have learned to SHOW UP and ASK for what I want!

We are the DREAM MAKERS. The name of our Mary Kay unit is the "Dream Makers, making dreams come true". I heard a song called A Million Dreams from the movie The Greatest Showman and the words talk about painting in vivid colors, not in pastels. That is now me.

What have I learned from my life so far? Not to accept fear – just do it till it feels natural. Strive for excellence because each step you take towards it improves you. Learn to look back to figure out how to do things differently and better, but do not dwell on that past. Never stop learning about and doing new things – grab onto new experiences. Be tenacious, flexible, and adaptable at all stages of your life. If I had not latched onto the new virtual aspect of our Mary Kay, I would have been left behind. Be willing to change your thinking and patterns in life no matter your age. I have learned to seize the moment because tomorrow is not promised.

ABOUT THE AUTHOR

Sandie Fuenty

Sandie Fuenty is a woman that is used to wearing many hats. Currently, she wears the hat of Independent Sales Director with Mary Kay Inc., Secretary of the Board of Officers of VeriDiva Women's Business Networking Group, Director of GSFE (Global Society for Female Entrepreneurs) Lake Elsinore/Murrieta/Wildomar chapter. She loves facilitating the monthly meetings, whether in person or Zoom, and helping other women broaden their sphere of influence.

She was born in the small town of Paris, Illinois, November 17, 1949. Both her parents had grown up in the surrounding farming communities. Her cousins still live there and every August a family reunion is held in Paris. When she was two, her family was transferred to Terre

Haute, Indiana where her dad worked for the Campbell Soup Company. The family again moved when she was in second grade to Cicero, Illinois for Campbell Soup. This was a big suburb of Chicago and a big move for the family. Occasionally on Saturdays she would get to take the "ell" downtown with her dad to help him work.

Sandie lived in Cicero until she met her husband, Jim and they moved to Bolingbrook, Illinois and then in 1980 moved to Southern California where they have stayed. They much prefer the California winters; she does miss seeing the snow, but not having to shovel or drive in it. The beaches of So Cal are the places she loves to go to replenish her mind and body.

Her background has been in administrative support in Corporate America, running the family's heating and air conditioning business and working out in the field until her husband's health required the closing of the business in 2014. She has been with Mary Kay Cosmetics for over 27 years. The priorities of Mary Kay Ash brought her into the company – faith first, family second, career third – and that the company believed in treating everyone by the Golden Rule. This atmosphere was quite different than corporate America and being a woman in the construction industry. August 1, 2020 (which happened to be her 49th wedding anniversary) she became an Independent Sales

Director with Mary Kay (top 2% of the company) with the help of her unit of 33 hand-picked ladies. They went on to qualify for the 2021 Chevy Malibu on September 1, 2020. What is amazing is that this was during the Pandemic when so many companies were floundering. Sandie says she owes it all to taking God as her partner in this business and grabbing on to the new virtual way of doing business. Quite a feat for a 71-year-old! Next goal is to reach Fabulous 50's with 50-unit members.

About the time of the closing of her husband's business, Sandie knew it was time to take a step back into the business world to promote herself. She entered the Network Marketing world. Little did she know how this would open so many doors. She learned to show up and ask. All that helped reawaken her business.

With the help and guidance of several mentors, she started writing for a local paper, wrote a chapter for an upcoming book and is working on her own manuscript.

She was a Board Member on the Dresses and Dreams Project for several years while it transitioned to a non-profit and is still active in the organization. She loves fulfilling her position of Secretary on the Board of Directors of the VeriDivas. Also, she plans fundraising events and fun activities to help Smile Train.

She has been presented many awards signed by two

Presidents, is an Ambassador and speaker representing the Mary Kay Charitable Foundation focusing on women's cancers and domestic violence. She has received Recognition Certificates from Senators, Congress, and local Charities and Organizations for her service.

Sandie and Jim have lived in Lake Elsinore since 2003 and watched it grow. They have 2 adult children and one precious granddaughter, Sophia (the apple of their eye). She is active in her church and for years has loved working with the four- and five-year old children. In her leisure hours, Sandie loves to read books, garden, spend time with family and friends and watch women grow. She loves to travel and can pack her suitcase within an hour's notice.

CHAPTER 12

THE GREATEST INVESTMENT

Terri Parker

As a child I would visit Dude, my Grandmother, who lived in a small logging town in Oregon. I loved spending my summers away from the bustle of living in the suburbs of Los Angeles and venturing through the woods of Keno, fishing off the Keno bridge, camping and horseback riding, learning how to appreciate the simple things in life. Unfortunately, the value of my Grandma Dude and those summers in the country, were not fully appreciated until well into my adult years. My hope in writing this Chapter, is that if even one young woman will be able to see the tremendous value and insight that her elders can bring, then I have accomplished what I wanted to accomplish. I realize now that I have Grandma Dude's determination, thought processes, strong will and her strong love of family. I wish I had appreciated her more when I was younger. Her home and little town were a refuge for me every summer.

My childhood was a typical childhood with one exception. When I was very young, the personal boundaries in my young life were dramatically and (so I thought) irreparably blurred. I used to feel it made me who I am. I do not feel that way anymore.

My personal boundaries were violated repeatedly by someone who was a member of the family. I unknowingly had choices. Being violated can either break a child to the point of no return, make that child a victim forever or that child can instinctively survive the confusing feelings and overcome them. I unknowingly chose the last option.

How I **overcame** those blurred boundaries made me who I am. I instinctively had to go through the process of remembering and confronting the abuser and the people whom I believed should have protected me. Not all outcomes were how I envisioned them. Fortunately, I was able to make peace with those loved ones who, while unaware of what was happening to me, were blamed by me, for their inability to protect me. I doubt they ever fully understood the dramatic effect on my life if those events of my childhood had not taken place. I had to make a decision. I chose to love them and keep them in my life except, of course, the abuser.

The revelation of this abuse and the chaos it caused for a time did not take place until I was well into adulthood.

Thank goodness, because the little girl that was me would not have been able to reconcile all that had happened during that time.

In my teenage years, my natural abilities in learning enabled me to focus on extra-curricular activities while keeping up the appearances of the studious and serious student. For the most part, I was able keep up the 4.0 grade point average without a lot of effort. This allowed me to pretend to be the person I wanted to be knowing deep down it was very far from the truth. I instinctively spent my time trying to overcome my own fears and insecurities. When someone did not like me, for whatever reason, it was devastating to me. I seemed to have always stopped short of succeeding in a lot of the areas that would have completely gotten me out of my comfort zone. Looking back, if I had taken that last step, my confidence would have blossomed. I would have been able to continue moving forward in whatever goal I pursued with the success that I craved but could not bring myself to achieve.

That is not to say that I did not succeed in most of the endeavors that I pursued. However, they were not life changing successes. I realize now that most of my successes in those early years had been in areas that I knew I could succeed in before I even started. Also, most of my pursuits included joining in social situations, team sports in elementary school, cheerleading and academic clubs in high school, junior college instead of a university etc. This was so that I could pursue success but did not necessarily have to be on my own and achieve it alone. Therefore, success was not all mine, but then neither was the failure. It was always a group effort as well as the individual effort. I believe that my competitiveness, of which I was unaware, overcame a lot of my shyness, low self-esteem and fears.

After a couple of years of going through junior college and still not knowing with certainty what I wanted to do with my life, I ended up in the job I took working part-time while going to college. As before, I started getting out of my comfort zone in college and subconsciously I chose to continue in the "temporary job" telling myself that the money and benefits worked for me. I settled for the work that was safe and that I knew I could do. I stayed in that job for 21 years. I realize now that I was not happy with the fact that I did not take the risks I needed to take to get where I wanted to be and get out of my comfort zone. I stayed where it was "comfortable".

Instead of finishing college, marriage and children came next (it was what was expected of me). I raised my children to pursue their own dreams, have each other's backs, and to always be there for each other no matter the circumstances. I developed friendships that still exist today. I made enough money to pay my bills and feed my family. I had health insurance to ensure their wellbeing. To everyone – friends, family, and husband – it looked as though I had everything together, and living a life that some envied.

One day when I came home from work, my daughter ran up to me and excitedly exclaimed that she and her brother were in a drive-by shooting. That day my whole world changed. It took the safety of my children or lack thereof, to awaken the Benefactor within me (a personality trait that is very strong according to the personality test I took later but I was unaware of at the time) and bring it to the forefront. As my children were always my priority, after 16 years in the same neighborhood, I uprooted my family and moved to a safer area. This was not an overnight thing. What I realize looking back is that there was no lack of self- confidence, no worry about my comfort zone, no fear of whether or not I was doing the right thing. My children needed to grow up in a safe environment and I needed to get them there.

I started my pursuit by finding the safe place for my children to grow up and then doing what was needed to be done to get there. This was all me. This was me stepping out of my comfort zone to get my children to safety no matter what. That was my focus. Even though they did not understand why I uprooted them, all that mattered to me was that *I* knew why, and I knew someday they would understand. I had made up my mind, and through my pursuit of becoming the person I want to be, I have learned the power of a decisive mind. The seemingly impossible can be accomplished simply because your mind is made up to do so. *I wish I had known this in my younger years.*

This one event and the events that ultimately followed are the beginning of my journey for finding my self-esteem and confidence to go for the dreams that I now allow to become my goals and ultimately my successes. This life is a journey and I have found that one by one I can tear down the insecurities and doubts that plagued my early years.

The lesson in this is to find what is most important to you. What is it that motivates you? Some people call it your "Why". I did not realize until after that moment that my greatest incentive for everything in my life is my children. All of whom are adults now. I am immensely proud of all of them. I also taught them to take that one extra step when they finished a task or assignment, to be sure it was complete and done right. Their father and I also taught them to stick together no matter what because no one else in this world are their sibling and no one will be there for them like they will be there for each other.

The path to my learning how to build confidence and self-esteem started with reading a book by Shad Helmstetter, "What to Say When You Talk to Yourself." I realized after reading this book that I was in charge of my thoughts, dreams, goals, emotions, successes, and failures. I could hide behind the people I surrounded myself with and never take responsibility for any of it. But I would truly never have the success that I was learning that I craved. I could also allow other people to dictate how I feel at any given moment. This was truly an eye-opening revelation and I decided to make my own feelings my top priority. That was how I could best take care of my family and take care of me. My children were older and much more self-sufficient. This allowed me to focus more on me for the first time ever! I became aware of the things I said to myself and things other people around me said. I made the necessary changes in my life in order to be the person I genuinely wanted to become instead of just pretending to be that person. I discovered that learning who I truly am is the main ingredient for becoming who I want to be. I invested in myself. I made mistakes along the way. But the mistakes get you to the successes. The mistakes teach you what you need to learn.

I learned I have personality traits that are more dominant than others. We all do. I have already referenced my Benefactor trait. I am also extremely competitive. In the same personality test I am an Olympian. I do not give up when I want something, even when it is not good for me. This is an instinct. I have learned to rein in my Olympian in under *that* circumstance! I am also a perpetual and rapid person. I would keep going and going until my body told me to stop by breaking down and forcing me to stay at home in bed. I have learned that I need to take the time to celebrate my achievements no matter how small and slow down when I need to. This is still a work in progress.

When I decided to change from my job of 20 years and take on a career as a Realtor, I was 40 years old. I just knew that I was not happy with the job I had been working for so long. I did not realize that making that decision to build my own business would help to lead me to the path I needed to achieve the goals and successes that I wanted. I also did not realize that it would lead me to the path of finding out who I am and what I wanted to achieve in my life. I read books, listened to tapes (those were the days before everything was readily available to download) and went to as many conferences as I was able to. I finally found a coach and mentor for both my business and my personal life. Since then, I have continued to peel away the layers of doubt and fear of leaving the boundaries of my comfort zone by continuing to read, watch webinars and go to conferences. My mentor taught me and countless others that investing in yourself is the best investment you will ever make. I believe that with all of my heart. Do not try to go through this life alone. Do not think you have all of the answers. You do not. You have to be open to constructive criticism of yourself by you. You also need a mentor. Work to constantly get out of your own way and out of your comfort zone. If you do not, you will stagnate and go nowhere. What I did not know was that I was internalizing the philosophies of the people I was learning from. It was starting to appear in the way I conducted myself both personally and professionally.

It is a surprising feeling when you discover how other people perceive you. A good friend of mine, Lisa, whom I met when we sat next to each other at a breakfast meeting for the Brokerage I was working for, (we are both Realtors) started talking at that breakfast and in my view, we became instant friends. I was amazed when later after becoming great friends, she told me of her feelings before getting to know me. In her view, she was amazed that I would talk with her. She told me when she first met me, she was very intimidated by me. I was incredulous. However, I have had several of my friends tell me that since then. My lack of confidence apparently never showed to others in my professional life.

Another lesson I have learned through investing in myself. I learn by exploring, by physically being there. Hence, that is one reason why I love to travel! I discovered this after I had gone to several different conferences in different cities that were short flights away from home. It seemed I learned more at those conferences than I did at the local ones. The distractions of daily life were far away while I was there. I started setting goals to travel to places that appealed to me. There were very few times that I did not reach that goal to be able to travel to those places!

I wish this had been something that I was taught in my younger years. Through this process of learning to write goals I learned that writing down your dreams and wishes changes them from dreams and wishes to goals that you can achieve. I first learned this in my early years as a Realtor. I had written my desires for the coming year. To me it was just an exercise that my Broker was making me do. It did not mean much to me. I did not keep them in front of me, I put them in a file in the desk drawer. A year later, I found them in the drawer and pulled out that list of desires. I had accomplished every one of them! That was the beginning of my true belief in myself. The belief that if I did invest in myself, I could achieve just about anything I wanted to achieve. Again, the power of a made-up mind.

Now I am not saying that everything will fall right into your lap. Most things will not. However if you are prepared and you are investing in yourself, when the opportunity arises for you to grab it (whatever "it" is) you will be ready for it! Do not be afraid to swim upstream when everyone else is floating with the tide. Find your own path and keep moving and growing. Make up your mind who and what you want to be so you can inspire others you love and those who will come after you. I hope I have.

ABOUT THE AUTHOR

Terri Parker

Terri Parker was born in Klamath Falls, Oregon, the middle child and only girl. When she was only two years old, her family move to and settled in San Gabriel Valley, a Los Angeles County suburb.

She spent her summers back in Keno, Oregon near Klamath Falls. This gave her a well-rounded perspective of the differences in the ways of life of two completely different lifestyles.

She states that she had the best of both worlds learning to fish, camp, horseback ride, herd sheep, and drive at a young age, water ski and enjoy all that country living has to offer during the summers, while growing up with all that suburban living had to offer the rest of the year.

Terri is a mother of three grown children and grandmother of 5 ages ranging from 5 months to 20 years.

She currently resides in Menifee, CA with her partner Sam. Her love of family, travel, and horseback riding are all contributing factors to the reasons that she loves helping families when they transition from and to their new homes. She loves seeing the excitement of first-time homebuyers when they get their keys to their new home. She has deep empathy for the widow/widower, when selling the home which he/she shared with the loved one, after that loved one is gone.

Her history of working in customer service for over 20 years enabled her to earn a living by intuitively understanding her clients and meeting their needs while always keeping their best interests as her top priority. This is one of the secrets to her success of working and growing her Real Estate business by referral.

Terri's free time consists of traveling to new destinations, spending time with her children and grandchildren, enjoying the local wineries of Temecula with Sam. She also enjoys socializing with friends and family, going to concerts, movies and the theater.

www.ingramcontent.com/pod-product-compliance
Lightning Source LLC
Chambersburg PA
CBHW040107120526
44589CB00039B/2770